Get "The stray dog" out -

Author
Tom Arild Fjeld

Get "The stray dog" out -

ISBN 978-82-93410-37-9

Get "The stray dog" out

Get "The stray dog" out -
Writer: Tom Arild Fjeld
Copyright Tom Arild Fjeld
Print: nr.1- 2016
ISBN 978-82-93410-37-9
Publisher Faith & Vision
Layout: Frank Håvik
Text: Times New Roman 13
Heading: Lucida Handwriting 18

Get "The stray dog" out -

Table of contents.

Chapter 4

The ungodly "Life philosophers"
Behind every word there's a
spirit.

Chapter 5

Communism
"Dig in"
It was no more talk about the
communism.
Karl Marx.
The Satanic idea – Communism.
A Christian became a God hater.
Lenin.
God deniers.
Communism – A Satanic attack
of dimensions.
It is not hard to see Satan and the
demons behind the politics.
Blessing and curse.

Chapter 6

Satan and the demons frontal
attack on the Christian west.
Religions.
Pantheism.
Christianity.
New Age thinking.
The so called New Age thinking.

Get "The stray dog" out

It was in south California New
Age started.
David Spangler.
The phenomenon Esalen Institute.
The phenomenon Esalen
originated in a warm Christian
home in Hamburg 100 years ago.
Esalen Institute, unite "the eternal
philosophy" from east and west.

Chapter 7

New Age and spiritism.
Spiritism foundation for
parapsychology
Spiritism and its history.
Theosophy.
Anthroposophy.
Philosophy.

Chapter 8

Santa Barbara in California
became mecca for the hippie
culture, and one of the centres for
New Age ideas.
When the hippie wave faded.
The other "river"
Esalen institute becomes a
legendary "house of growth"
Jesus revival.

Get "The stray dog" out -

Chapter 10

Are you as a Christian on the offense or are you a lazy one.
It is war in the world of the spirit, and it will last until Jesus returns.
Again – the victory is ours, use it.
There is no mediator between you and Christ.
Every soldier is trained for war.
The provisional government's meeting in Bucharest, Romania.
The Indian guru woman in Bucharest.
Spreading of the Reincarnation-gospel in the west.
Put an end to the painful circle of reincarnation.

Chapter 11

The unconscious, but determined attempt to combine the two spiritualities – which is eternally impossible.
Spiritualism.
The spiritual existence.
The evil spirits manipulations, lies and deceit.
John of God, the medium from South America.

A healer is made.
Chosen.
Into the demonic service.
The beginning of bondage.
Bound strongly in the
soul/personality.
Here we see the speech of lie and
confusion.
As born again humans we must
know the scripture, the Bible.
And learn to live and walk in the
Spirit, and to exercise the ability
to test spirits.
Do you see the gravity.
Demons go both ways with
sickness.
The medium John of God.
The demons puts on and takes
away sickness.
You experience freedom from
sickness for a while.
There is not health no matter the
cost.
The demons rejoice when they
torment humans.
It is demons who appear.
Spiritism and its history.
The death of the spiritist pope.

Get "The stray dog" out -

The creed of the medium John of God.

John of Gods wife Ana says:

Chapter 12

Satan builds a network across the world.

"Altar call of Satan".

People accept "Satan's altar call" and they let all the different alternatives become their lives leaders.

Alternative exhibition.

Chapter 13

There are many ways to draw near to Satan – Both consciously and unconsciously.

Satan worshipers.

Satan worship in Stavanger.

The ring of fire.

Exorcising demons.

The woman with a spirit if divination on Likoni island.

The leading witchdoctor of Zanzibar.

Foreign languages.

Satan worshippers: The dead gets life. Black mass.

Chapter 14

Ways to get bound by Satan and demons – consciously and unconsciously.
An eternal conglomeration.
Witchcraft is tightly bound to astrology and evil spirits.
Satan and the demons name and number are of no importance.
Nature religion.
Anthropologists.
Among the nature people.
The difference between religion and magic.
In the nature religion we see the front runner to the western spiritism and we recognize animism.
Animism.
The term animism was originally a part of a philosophical theory.
That's why every human seek its master.
Spiritist séance.
Everything spiritual has its author.

Get "The stray dog" out

Chapter 15

Nature religion you can find in
different religions such as
occultism and spiritism.
Nature religion.
Anthropologists.
With the nature people.
The difference between religion
and magic.
In the nature religion we see the
front runner to the western
spiritism and we recognize
animism.
Animism.
The term animism was originally
a part of a philosophical theory.
That's why every human seek its
master.
Spiritist séance.
Everything spiritual has its
author.
I want to mention some, about the
big religions today.
Explaining appendix.
Were Marx, Stalin, Hitler and
Mao involved in the occult?

Chapter 16

The occult – Islam's hidden side.
Muhammad.

Chapter 17

You shall have no other gods
before me, and you shall not
make yourself any carved image
or any likeness.
Animism.
The origin of spirits.
The relation with the spirits.
Contact with spirits.
The animism's invisible bondage
of people in the western world.
Fetishism.
The beginning of nature religion.
1000 years from the fall of man
to the start of Hinduism.
We see clearly that before Christ
came, worshiping of false idols
had been in the world for almost
4000 years.
The burning of fetishes on
crusades around the world.
The demons reveal themselves
quickly and they come out with
loud screams.

It is difficult for most people to take witchcraft seriously.

Chapter 18

Witchdoctors and warlocks.
They gave themselves completely to Satan.
Many conceives warlocks as frauds.
Cut the head off a snake and whip people with the body of the snake.

Chapter 19

The biggest spiritual crisis in 2000 years is here now.
Mankind under attack.
The church under attack.
Not every supernatural thing that happens is the Lords doing.
How Satan and the demons gets to use us.
The occult harvest – Satan and the demons got their scythes out for harvest.

Chapter 20

Spirituality or the flesh.

"In the spirit and under the
anointing"
Pastor and teacher.
Get in the position of the spirit.
What is the answer?

Chapter 21

Is everything impossible? - Yes,
if we don't repent and believe.
Will Jesus return?
It is only one guarantee for Jesus
soon coming – who can stop the
occult onslaught?
A new dark age.
The victory can come sooner than
you think.
We must get into position.

Chapter 22

God's breakthrough power in
Jesus Christ, Your foundation for
victory.
What is the most important
message in the world?
How did they manage to do that?
Meeting with the students in
college.

Get "The stray dog" out -

It has never been power in the cross, but only in the man that hung there. (Gal 3, 13).
How will you get a faith like that?
The change in the circumstances – will always start with you.
What do you talk about? What is your spirit filled with?
The negative got turned to positive in the situation.
Everything impossible becomes to us a possibility.

Chapter 23

Throwing out demons.
Got into this service without seeking it.
Demons gets drawn towards The Holy Spirit.
If the Demons reveal themselves to you, then you can throw them out.
We command the demons to come out in Jesus Name! 1 time – Not 2 times.
We live under the new covenant.

"Religious Christians" can walk
around in a "demon free world"
with luck.
Are you born again?
Have you ever been baptized with
The Holy Spirit, fire and power?
Do you have The Holy Spirit's
fire and power active in your life?
Are you not born again?

Chapter 24

Everyone that are saved can
throw out demons.
How to throw out demons.
I bind every demon I meet today,
in Jesus name.
You demon, you unclean spirit –
Get out in the name of Jesus.
Resist Satan.
Satan knows me.

Chapter 25

The inner backyard and the street
outside – the spirit world inside
you and around you.

Chapter 26

Reflection

Get "The stray dog" out -

Chapter 27
20-20 vision.
Mass healing and mass
deliverance.

The preacher and the world evangelist Tom Arild Fjeld,

has travelled all over the world and preached
the gospel since he was a young man at the
age of 21. He had never planned to become a
Christian or a preacher, but God had other
plans. He has travelled in more than 58
nations. The burden on his heart has been to
reach the unreached and move in where no
one has been before him. In his meetings the
crowds had been from 100 to 100 000
people.
Deliverance from demons, healing of the
sick and salvation to rebirth has been his
banner. Beside that he has a strong teaching
ministry whom he use everywhere. He is
also a author of a big no. of books.
The prophetic view in his life, is easy to
obtain in his preaching, teaching and books.

He is a typical "proclaimer" a herald in his proclamation of the gospel as an evangelist. As a teacher it shines through his revelation in the word.
He is teaching and instruction people who are carrying on a call in their heart. He can do it in a practical way, because of his long life experience in the field. How they can take hold on the different types of situations in the spiritual realms in the ministry.

Evangelist Rune Larsen

Preface

I have written several books the last months.
It is something I did not plan to do. But
during a live broadcast on TV, I got a request
from a caller to write a book about prayer. I
then wrote the book "Pray through – Prayer
in the deep". When the writing process had
started, I began on another book. Then
another. The last book I wrote this round is
the one you have in your hands.
In all of my books, my wish is that you will
get a full understanding and clarity in
important spiritual truths in the Bible, and
practical uses of them.
Likewise I want you to understand the world
that we live in, with all its beliefs. Not only
the religions, but also all the other
alternatives. What lies as a bearing
foundation, a failing one at that, for all
religions and alternatives, is a spiritual
world. Religions and the alternatives seek
the metaphysical or the supernatural and
spiritual, without understanding what that
involves. Religions put a god's name on their
religion, while those who are in the
alternative speak about energy, force, angels,
vibrations etc. In the alternative we can also
see that Hinduism and Buddhism have some
place, even though it is not often spoken

about. Within New Age one can see Hinduism and Buddhism influence, but more of it comes from spiritism, occultism, mediums and channelling. It is a spiritual world behind the created one. Natural science has only given us answers to some of the physical and material questions in the universe. But today leading scientists in that field acknowledges that behind the physical universe, there is a spiritual reality. So there is a spiritual world behind and over the physical and material world. This is old news for me and you. The Bible has taught us this. Dr. Carlo Rubbia, who got the Nobel peace price in physics in the year 1984, confirms that there is a spiritual world which goes through and stands above the physical world. We can say congratulations on catching up. The knowledge of the spiritual world he will only get after being born again. It won't help much discovering this or that. Our God Yahweh is the creator of it all, and He sent his Son Jesus Christ as ransom for our sins. The spiritual world is just as much our home as the physical. But here we have to humble ourselves and believe the whole Bible and Jesus Christ as our Lord and Saviour. Centred in his reconciliation work, and His

Get "The stray dog" out

victorious, holy blood. That is the only way into this amazing world.

My experience with Christians through 40 years, is that they lack understanding of common basic Christian truths. Truths which normally should be known to everyone in a living Christian society. Our people are spiritually perishing, because they don't have knowledge or experience. If you want to live as a Christian, but have almost none foundational truths in your life. You will easily become a prey for the wrong influence.
One will then easily accept false information about the Biblical message, and be led astray. Here again we can see without a shadow of a doubt that Satan and the demons are entering the Christians play field. This is a reality that we see daily in the western world now, stronger than ever before.

Listen to what Jesus said in Matt 22, 29 "You are wrong, because you know neither the Scriptures nor the power of God."

What's dangerous about the folk religiosity is the fact that, despite its blurriness, it represents a perception of what Christianity is. The folk religiosity got its catechism. Simplified in many ways, but it has its doctrines. The high and the depth is missing, the shades and nuances, contrast and tension, light and darkness – all of this disappears, but the unclear greyness which remains constitutes a form of a Christian view. When things get a little hairy in life, this religiosity comes to use. The folk religiosity is alive, it is most certainly not a dead religiosity. Its curse is its distance from the living centre of faith. And it is filled with unclarity that comes from distancing oneself from faith. When there's question about what Christianity is, the folk religiosity gets activated.

Opinions about this question is characterized by the same lack of interest of clarity. If someone believes in God, then he is a Christian. If he also lives a morally upright life, then its ear ringing unfair to say that he is anything but a good Christian.

When you read this book you will understand why I wrote this, dear friend. God bless you on the journey through this book. I hope you will find much of that you have been looking for.

Get "The stray dog" out -

Remember! Much of what I write is from literature which deals with different subjects I touch, this I use only so that you will get clarity in the matter. Then you can step forward in spiritual strength and understanding of the situation.

More than ever in the history of man, there is need for a strong, pulsating and living faith in Jesus Christ, and His reconciliation on Calvary for all mankind.

"The Gospel is the power of God for salvation to everyone who believes" Says Paul in the letter to the Romans. (1, 16)

We must step forward in the power of the Spirit, with the gift of the Spirit in our lives, and stand victorious after we have defeated everything in our Lord Jesus name. (Eph 6, 13)

As you read this book, you will get a more broad understanding of where we are in the spiritual picture, and what you can contribute to in that connection. There is a spiritual world and we have to deal with it accordingly. You see how Satan and his demons have infiltrated the society and the Church.

I will mention a little about the different
faiths, just enough for you to get an
understanding of the seriousness.
I will also here just mention some about the
new religious movements in Scandinavia.
They are as follows:

ACEM meditation movement (free
Hinduism) started in 1966

Ahmadiyya-islam, founded by an Indian guy
in 1899

Ananda-marga with roots in Hinduism. It
came to Norway early in the 70's by an
Indian guy named Baba.

Anthroposophy. Rudolf Steiner presents
himself as an occult spiritual science.

Bahia which originated in Islam.

Children of God came to Norway in the 70's
with David Moses as leader. They play a lot
on sex.

Christian Science. Christian science means
the science which lies as a base for
Christianity.

The United family. God sends the third
Adam which is the leader of this sect,
Myung Moon.

Divine light mission. They came to
Scandinavia in the early 70's. The movement
got roots in Hinduism and was brought here
by a young Indian guy born in 1957. (More
about him later in the book)

Eckankar. Founded by an American named
Paul Twichell, their practice comes from
India. They practice bi-location, it means to
be in two places at the same time.

International society for Krishna. They use
orange monk garments, shave their heads
and have thin ponytails hanging down from
the upper part of the back of their heads.

Jehovah witnesses. Founded by Charles Taze
Russel (1852-1916) He had not planned to
start his own organization, but because of all
his written works and the watchtower which
he wrote the first edition to in 1879, The
Bible and tract company "watchtower" got
started.

"Kristensamfundet" With roots connected to Rudolf Steiner.

Mormons. Founder Joseph Smith (Born.1805) When he was 18 years old he claimed to receive 2 gold tablets from an angel named Maroni. He said it was the book of Mormon. He died in 1844.

New Age. Which I write about later in this book.

Rajneeshism (Bhagwan Shree Rajneesh) He has had a monastery in Oregon, USA and a big ashram in Poona, India. He was a professor in philosophy and meditation was the most important thing for him and his many women. He died in the 90's.

Scientology Church. Many knows about this church. They teach: Your mental illness is not real, it's all in your mind conquer your mind and you are Healthy.

Subud. With out of the body experiences. (let all the senses flow and just listen inwards.) They had offices in Oslo since 1958, its own Gurdjifeff department in Norway.

Get "The stray dog" out -

The Theosophical society. Which is strongly influenced Indian religiosity. I will write more about Transcendental meditation later in the book.

Way international. They got many parallels to Children of God.

Worldwide church of God. Founded in USA by Herbert Armstrong in 1839. He claimed to be the only one to preach true Christianity after the Acts of the Apostles.

Something that is recurring in all religious sects, is that the reconciliation has not taken place, that Jesus did not die on the cross and that He is not Gods Son. For them, it doesn't exist any precious blood of Jesus Christ, Gods own Holy blood, which takes away the sin of the world.
That which is the most important thing in the Bible, is to all the sects to be counted as a lie. Look how Satan has blinded this world. But now we come! Friends, we must stand up and conquer Satan and the demons, with the Victory of Jesus Christ today!
We have to do it now, so that the world can get the living testimony about Jesus Christ, and so that he can return. Do you

understand? We must be much much more radical and bold. Just press on, now!

There are other sects or religious societies I could have mentioned, but I think this will be enough. Think about it! Those I have mentioned have spiritual influence in the west. These are groups that Christians might not have heard of. We can see Satan and the demons wicker around the world. They started just after the fall of Adam, and have built on it little by little. The demons have spun their webs into this world for almost 6000 years, but the victory is ours!

Don't be frightened by what you read in this book, let it be to you information and inspiration, to carry on as a warrior of Jesus Christ. This will lead you into new areas in the spirit.

My dear wife has edited all the books as I wrote them. She is an irreplaceable, encourager, a true inspiration and supporter.

Tom Arild Fjeld

Get "The stray dog" out

Chapter 1

"Stray dogs"

I grew up on Thorshov in Oslo, along the river Aker. It was here all the small industry in the city got built up, and started the financial growth. Little by little the city grew out of the rookie problems and poverty. People did not have a lot of money in those days.

I grew up in an apartment building on Torshov. One thing that was special about the apartment buildings at that time, was that they all had backyards. The backyards were for the apartment owners only and nobody else. In the backyards there were drying racks for every apartment owner. In the basement we had wooden washtubs for the residents to wash their clothes. There were also a room with a big wooden mangle for use after the clothes were dried.

Next to the entrance door to the backyard, there was a big hatch. It was "the poop hatch" (were "Pudritten" as they were called, came and collected the poop,) "Pudritten" was the part of the department of sanitation which came and collected the waste from the toilets that were installed in the hallways in different floors. I was luxury, we had gotten

the latrines inside small rooms in the
hallway. There were pipes in every floor
leading down to the poop hatch.
Beyond the drying racks in the backyard,
there was an "oasis". Which the ladies used
as garden. They took care of flowers and
vegetables which blossomed and bore fruit.
There they grew fine tomato plants alongside
the walls, it was a great sight. When the sun
was shining down there during summer, it
was like a paradise. Yes a paradise, until the
stray dogs dug up the bones they had hidden.
Then it looked like a freshly plowed field.
It was so wonderful there in the backyard –
except the city pigeons, "stray dogs", stray
cats and rats, which were as big as the stray
cats. And sometimes we even got visited by
badgers. The city pigeons pooped on
everything in the backyard, they lived in the
rain gutters. It would often happen that we
got hit with poop from the birds flying
through the air. The stray cats used to piss
and shit all over the backyard also, and they
were always meowing and chasing the
pigeons. The stray dogs were out of control,
against them we were powerless. The rats
were dangerous, they would bite if we were
not careful. When we saw one coming we
would try to catch it. When the badger

showed up we would stay inside. If we were to try to catch the badgers, we would put on boots, then push as much coal into them as possible. If the badgers bit us, they would let go when they heard the crushing of the coal. One thing that wasn't so smart, but it happened with the best intentions by the ladies in the flats. Was that the food which were leftovers, they gave to the dogs, cats and rats down in the backyard.

Some of the backyards in the city looked like zoos, it were those who had a bakery in them. Here it were treats for all the "wild" animals under the sky. There were small industries in every backyard.

The backyards were our place of safety and peace, but in the midst of all the positive, there were elements who were out to destroy the harmony.

It was not only the "stray dogs", but also other enemies who wanted to destroy the life we had, as we saw it, we who lived in these apartment buildings. Thieves came during the nights to steal. What was left or forgotten outside would be gone the following day. This was life and we loved it. But we had to protect ourselves, no matter the cost.

Get the devilry out of your backyards "oasis"

We did all we could to keep the backyard free from all these "hostile" elements which came. As the years passed we also adapted some way to all the things happening in the backyard. We learned to live with the things we couldn't get rid of, even if it bothered us. The stray dogs dug up the flowerbeds, and they buried things we didn't want there. This happened often, it was always struggle for the territory.

Do you have an inner backyard, and does it contain something that should not be there?

As it were in the city I grew up in, the physical world. We can easily draw parallels to what's happening in the spiritual world, inside us. The basement is a great picture of the spiritual life. There in the basement nothing could enter. It were only those things we wanted to have there that came inside. The backyard was just like our personality, our soul. Here things could enter if we did not keep watch and guard the territory. Through the bodily senses our soul gets contact with the world around us. It is like the women looking down onto the street below through their windows. Out there in our universe. Out into the circumstances of our lives. The windows become like our eyes. They become senses which sends impressions into the soul, into our personality. Here you can be bound by demons, in your soul. It is just like the women we called "walking flowerpots", they went from window to window, behind the curtains, so they could spy on people. One lady we called "The dry spruce". She went from one entryway to another, and watched what people were doing. These people were bound by their behaviour. In the same way the demons got power to form our personality and give us trouble, once they have entered. "The walking flowerpot" and "The dry spruce" could not stop doing this, they were bound by the behaviour. This cannot happen in people's spirit. In the spirit it will only happen if we willingly let demons inside, just as no strangers came down in the basement.

Get "The stray dog" out -

Chapter 2

The demons are a reality.
Demons are something we cannot see with
the physical eye, they are of another
dimension. In a human eye there are
something I for the sake of simplicity will
call "rods", which there are 8 of. The "rods"
let us see black, white and colours.
Cats got only 2 "rods", which leaves them to
only see black and white. They are missing
the colour dimension.
In a human there is a dimension we don't
have "observation rods" for, namely the
spiritual dimension. To get these "rods" in
place is possible, but only for a human that is
a new creation in Jesus Christ. Which is born
again and have Jesus as their Lord. In other
words a person who is saved. These extra
"rods" are of course not in the eyes, but in
the spirit. If this is in place, then it is the
Lordship of the Word, the Lordship of Christ
which has to get its place and be established
in our lives. Then we can little by little get
closer to a life with understanding and
knowledge to the spiritual dimension
through revelation of Gods written Word,
The Bible.

Jesus said it so describing to his disciples
"But if it is by the Spirit of God that I cast
out demons, then the kingdom of God has
come upon you." (Matt. 12, 28)

Jesus had that element in Him which let him
see the spiritual world, which the disciples
did not have.
You can start to live consciously in that
world if you like. This opportunity has been
given us in Jesus Christ. You can train up
this overview of what's going on in the spirit
world.

Ephesians. 6, 12 "For we do not wrestle
against flesh and blood, but against the
rulers, against the authorities, against the
cosmic powers over this present darkness,
against the spiritual forces of evil in the
heavenly places."

Col. 2, 15 "He disarmed the rulers and
authorities and put them to open shame, by
triumphing over them in him."

You see, in here you can come with the
victory of Christ in your life. Understanding,
insight and The Holy Spirit's dominion in the
name of Jesus.

Get "The stray dog" out

Chapter 3

You stand before God alone.
I have been a Christian for 40 years.
Through those years I have observed
something that has been static, something
that has always been. It is the Christians (I
choose to call them that), state of mind. I
mean the Christians total lack of spiritual
growth. It has not been a lack of speeches,
teachings or bible schools, but the case is –
how is it with you? You and your personal
relationship with Christ Jesus? Have you
grown into a man's maturity, and teach
others what you see and know, like the Bible
says we all in time shall be able to do?
You have maybe gone to a church for several
years, or been a "Christian" without
belonging to any congregation, only visiting.
Maybe been in a fellowship which met
now and then. All this is good.
But are you a new creation? **Have you been
born again? Are you saved? Do you have
a 100% assurance that you are?
Do you know if you are baptized with The
Holy Spirit's fire and power? Do you
know if your tongues is The Holy Spirit
speaking through you? Or is it something
you have made up yourself?**

I don't write this to frighten you, but to motivate/wake you up to a new, stronger, determined, convincing faith and a life in the power of The Holy Spirit.

We have to stop and reflect on where we stand today. We stand by a separation point in history, what will we do about it?

If we believe the message of the Bible and want to follow it, then you will understand and do what I talk about here.

It was in Antioch that those who believed in Jesus Christ and his atonement, for the first time got called Christians.

It was the heathen that called them Christians, because they looked so much like Jesus Christ. The right name for the born again is "The believers of Jesus Christ and His atonement on Calvary". I don't want to call myself Christ like that can other people do.

You can't blame the pastor or the church.

There is nothing that lies in the light of the day more than exactly this according to the message of the Bible that we all stand before Christ alone. There has been many excuses here. The Pastor is not good enough, the Church is not good enough. But the question

Get "The stray dog" out -

is: Are you good enough? We all stand
before The Lord alone, and the responsibility
before Him is ours ALONE. That is one
thing we cannot escape. Do you want to
grow in Christ, then you have to get here.
Christ is your saviour, you have to stand
responsible unto Him alone. If you want to
live victorious with Him, Then everything
have to be sacrificed for Him.

**You are weak, so it's probably good for
you to become a Christian.**
This is an opinion that has come from the
enemies of Christianity through the ages.
This is not a wise opinion, I would say this is
a foolish opinion. The truth is the opposite,
to live as a non-believer is easy, its peanuts.
It's just to cheer with the happy people,
follow the opinions and mind-set of the
masses, whichever way that will go. To keep
on walking in a joyful madness, with a smile
on your face, towards the eternal damn
nation.
Think, a life without a relation to Him who
created you and made plans for you. A
creator who loves you above all, He loves
you so much that He gave his Son as ransom
for your life.

A life as a believer in Jesus Christ and his atonement is not for "sissies"
To just go with the flow takes no willpower, it goes on its own. To go against the flow requires determination, and it builds up a new strength in all areas in your life.
You can become a "Giant" with The Lord if you like. Being a "sissy" who hides behind everyone else won't do you any good then. Being a "sissy" who blames everyone else won't do you any good then. Being a "sissy" who agrees with the masses no matter what they present as truth won't do you any good then.
Here you got to show power, will and boldness! You say: I want to be "a Giant of The Lord" a giant in Gods army. I will stand by Christ no matter what the world says. I pledge allegiance to Christ no matter what.

Matthew 17, 2-8
And he was transfigured before them, and his face shone like the sun, and his clothes became white as light. And behold, there appeared to them Moses and Elijah, talking with him. And Peter said to Jesus, "Lord, it is good that we are here. If you wish, I will make three tents here, one for you and one for Moses and one for Elijah. "He was still

Get "The stray dog" out -

speaking when, behold, a bright cloud overshadowed them, and a voice from the cloud said, "This is my beloved Son, with whom I am well pleased; listen to Him." When the disciples heard this, they fell on their faces and were terrified. But Jesus came and touched them, saying, "Rise, and have no fear." And when they lifted up their eyes, they saw no one but Jesus only.

This is our only salvation that Christ becomes our everything. Choose Christ as your everything before it's too late for you.

Get "The stray dog" out ·

Chapter 4

The ungodly "Life philosophers"
Life philosophy's history the last 200 years,
or should we say death philosophy's history.
In the 18th and 19th century the society
screamed for change, because the church and
the royal autocracy ruled over the human
mind and repressed the human rights. That
which came then, and contributed to our
modern life philosophy, threw the baby out
with the bathwater. Most of the philosophers
that came, hated God. Which shows that they
believed in Him. It had to be a God to hate.
They mocked Christianity or denied the
spiritual dimension. Approximately 250
years ago the modern human history began.
Around the year 1750 "the intellectuals" who
since then have influenced the world's way
of thinking, an started rebelling against that
times authorities. But the so called
"intellectuals", who were to change the
world and give mankind new values and life
rules, did they give us the right life
philosophies? The fruits of this philosophy
mix, which became the foundation for our
society, has shown that they must have been
unpleasantly mistaken.

All the life philosophers that came had one
thing in common, they were against God and
against Christianity. God's existence and the
problem of the evil one were denied. They
only believed in the human. Citizenship,
Christianity, society and public morality, got
the blame for all evil. These people denied
and excluded a basic foundation in our life
existence. All the great truths in the universe
are simple, for an example the law about
bearing fruit. Everyone knows that the
quality of the tree is known by the fruit it
produces. When we now in the new
millennium see what these "intellectuals"
life mix has brought us of separation
tendencies and collapses in east and west,
there is time for us to ask questions.
Everybody knows that "of the fruit you
know the tree", "everything becomes like its
master" and "the apple doesn't fall far from
the tree". Most of the "intellectuals" that
formed our world over the last 200 years,
have been atheists and left-winged. (As far
as this word is used back in history).
But these "intellectuals" were "enlightened"
and community oriented people. They had
knowledge of the Bible, and could there have
found out what the Gospel stood for. But still
most of them hated God and were enemies of

Get "The stray dog" out -

Christianity. They rejected its morals and created their own.

Why remove Jesus and the whole morale universe for family and marriage from the public Norway? **It is due to the philosophers**, who took over the mind-set and the ideological hegemony in our universities, especially after the year 1968. This became the consequence of not doing what Gods Word, the Bible teaches us.

Listen to what Paul said in 2.Cor. 10,4-5 For the weapons of our warfare are not of the flesh but have divine power to destroy strongholds. We destroy arguments and every lofty opinion raised against the knowledge of God, and take every thought captive to obey Christ,

You see? Every word has a power behind it, a spirit behind it. Either it is The Holy Spirit, Gods Spirit, or its Satan's and the demons evil spirits. The conquering tools have been given us in Christ Jesus, which we until now have not taken fully advantage of.

Behind every word there's a spirit.
Students who take an education, take control over political parties, administrations on

every level in public Norway and our schools. In a twinkling of an eye the Cultural Revolution was over.

Satan's wicker has started to tighten, but friends, the victory is ours in Christ Jesus! We just have to KNOW what we are up against, we got to know our enemy. We can defeat our enemy, Satan, in Jesus name, if we just prepare our spiritual weapons in the spiritual world. This is what this book is all about.

The world got fooled on every level by the philosopher's theoretical thoughts. Not practical and well tested thoughts which have strength. And also by the zeitgeist, which is a word we easily use. Zeitgeist – what is it? Zeitgeist is Satan's spirit, the one that tries to conquer the whole world.

Young people in student environments without the experiences of life, are easy preys for the zeitgeist, The thoughts of the philosophers, Satan's spirit. This is the reality. Because of philosophers strong influence in universities, in media and in churches, Jesus was taken out of the constitution may 21th 2012. We became a secular state. Secular states have until now in the history become " monster states".

Get "The stray dog" out -

"The only thing that can save us from the totalitarian danger, is that we turn back to our Christian heritage and the ten commandments", said the french new philosopher Levy.

The philosophy reprogrammed people's minds and brought brainwashing into the schools. The victory of the philosophy is made by using stealth technology that would be the hide-it-method. Just like our F-35 jet-fighters from USA becomes "invisible", when they attack, the philosophy becomes invisible on our radars. The battle can be won, but only in the invisible world were the enemy is. Satan uses the invisible technique, and so do we. We have the eternal, conquering, invisible technique, namely Jesus victory on Calvary, which was heard all over the spiritual world, and defeated Satan and the demons once and for all eternity! This invisible weapon has been given to you in Jesus Name! Use it!

I will now mention some of Satan's tools which has been essential to destroy mankind. They are all so called philosophers, not all well known. After reading about these, you would ask yourself, who is not a philosopher?

Voltaire Exalted the human sense as a new god, And believed in the liberating power of the enlightenment (age of reason). This is call intellect. Hmm...
He did everything he could to defeat The Bible in favour of the secular humanism, and its interpretation of reality.

Rousseau taught, contrary to The Bible, that the human is naturally good. Society has destroyed the human and made it evil. Therefore the State got to be like a father, raising his children to solve all problems, by creating a "new human" through school and the State's parenting. Here we have another smart guy, yeah yeah.

Charles Darwin dosed the philosophic materialism and taught that matter was before the spiritual, (clever guy), and not that the spiritual was before matter, as most natural scientists now believe.

Karl Marx Taught that religion is opium for the people. He preached to every worker, farmer, and all the earths proletarian about his "communist paradise". But he himself had never put his foot inside a factory, mine, industrial workplace or on a farm. He had

Get "The stray dog" out

never lived oppressed. He lived his whole life in Western Europe and died in London.

Nietzsche did not only attack Christianity, but also the Christian moral about love and compassion. He called it "slave morality" He raged against all values in his struggle to bring forth the new human "the übermensch", who lived beyond "good and evil" talk about dreams.

Bertrand Russell our times great "apostle of peace" discarded the belief in God. He taught that the answer to all the mysteries in the universe could be solved by human intellect. His doctrine was "We don't believe in God, but we believe in the human supremacy". How proud, arrogant and foolish can a person become?

Jean Paul Sartre Supported the violent revolution and bragged about Stalin, Castro and Mao. He was just as much antichrist as he was anti American and anti De Gaulle. He taught that the human creates its own life contents and life course, by daring to free itself from all values, and make a rebellion against the established society. This existentialism planted seeds in young cultural revolutionists, and in those who wanted to live unrestrained.

Mao's "Philosophical and political" experiment cost 100 million Chinese lives, when the drug addicted, sex crazed, atheistic, uncultivated country son, fooled the intellectuals and radicals of the west.

With "Mao's little red" he created the biggest holocaust in the world, in his own country. I remember well back in secondary school and high school, that some of my fellow students had a red Mao badge on their lapel, and "Mao's little red" in their pocket. This happened simultaneously as ML (Marxist Leninists) were popular in politics among some of the left wing radicals.

This was a short time before the flood of gurus from India, the Age of Aquarius and New Age. This was in the middle of the 60's. Everyone that have bodily senses to register with and a brain to think with, would be able to understand why these totalitarian leaders of mankind – now in the new millennium, are considered as fallen gods by millions.

Get "The stray dog" out -

The modern society which lived out their philosophies and sees the results today, found out that: "All things becomes like its master" and "the apple doesn't fall far from the tree"

Get "The stray dog" out -

Chapter 5

Communism

There are so many things you can be part of during your childhood, this is also my case. I had from early childhood the spiritual elements upon me, demons followed me until the day I got saved. Another thing I got introduced to, was communism.

It was no choice of mine, but it just happened. My father's twin brother got married into a known communist family in Norway, right after World War 2. They ran propaganda about the glory in Soviet Union, and the ideal nation Romania. Both of these named areas were nations in tragedy if you look at how they were governed.

The summer of 1966, when I was done with primary school, I was offered a trip to Czechoslovakia by the Norwegian communist party. This was 2 years before the Russian invasion. I and several other teenagers would for a month be guests of the Czechoslovakian communist party. (It was right after my arrival back home from Czechoslovakia, that I ruined my left eye). In Czechoslovakia we travelled around as a delegation for a month. We were together as guests with other teenagers from the

Scandinavian countries, including Finland and European countries in general.

I noticed many big crucifixes, on almost all the farms in the countryside, without paying much attention to it. We attended a lot of communist propaganda meetings. I got to see communism in its right element, and it did not impress me. I had no interest in it, and partook only for the sake of the trip. I was as mentioned together with youth from several European countries, which were to be future communist leaders. Maybe they also had hopes with me also, but God had other plans.

"Dig in"

When the meals were served, I got a new experience. Here it was no prayer or song for the food, here they all yelled with one voice "Dig in" There wasn't much respect for either God or the food in that yell. Before this trip to Czechoslovakia, I had also been to a Scandinavian summer camp at Rena in Norway, arranged for potential communist youth. It was communist propaganda all the time. And for a period of time I attended the communist scouts, which were called "The Pioneers". To me this became nothing more than fun experiences, and nothing more than that.

Get "The stray dog" out

It was no more talk about the communism.
The leaders of these trips and camps did nothing but drink, talk about communism and deny Gods existence in the evenings, when all the youngsters had gone to rest. So this is what I got out of communism, and all their praise of other ideal communist nations, which of course were miss placed.
When I many years later came back to Norway from my first campaign meetings in Romania (and building of orphanage), I told the communists in my family about the results of communism there. After that it was no more talk about the communism.

Karl Marx.
Karl Marx, born may 5th 1818, in Trier, was a Jewish ancestry, with rabbis both on the fathers and the mother's side of the family. He came from a relatively wealthy family. He became Christian early in his youth, and studied the Bible a lot during his years in college. He belonged to the Russian orthodox part of Christianity, I have no idea if he was saved or not.
On his exam papers from college it stated that he had good knowledge about religion. He had good knowledge about Christianity

and its history. A man named Moses Hess
got him convinced that communism was the
only right way.

The Satanic idea – Communism.
It was in the year 1841. Karl Marx wrote in a
letter to his father: "A curtain has fallen, my
holiest of holies has been torn apart, and new
gods has to be installed" This was the 10th
November 1837. He who had declared Christ
in his heart, for him it was no longer so.
He now hated all gods and all talk about
God. He was willing to become the man who
kicked God out. Socialism was the bait used
to attract proletarians and the intellectuals, to
get them to embrace this Satanic idea –
communism.
The Soviet Union had in its early years this
slogan: "Let us rid this planet of capitalism
and rid the heaven of God". When the
communist revolution broke out in Paris
1871, Communard Florence declared: "Our
enemy is God, hatred towards God is the
beginning of wisdom".

A Christian became a God hater.
Karl Marx laid as a foundation for
communism, the origin of this blind hatred
towards God. This again brought Satan and

the demons strong approach through this person, and out to the followers of this new manifesto. And eventually all over the world. He who in his childhood and youth was a Christian. In 1835 he wrote an essay for an exam, named "The union of believers with Christ according to John 15, 1-14" He wrote several Christian writings. The first one was a comment to the gospel of John.

Fall 1835 Karl Marx begins his studies, first in Bonn then from 1836 in Berlin. Already now it looks like he started to doubt Christianity. In 1837, Karl Marx became a member of "The Doctor club" in Berlin. Then it became obvious that he had parted with Christianity. The club was made up by a group of "young Hegelians". The members were political liberal, and considered an atheistic criticism of Christianity as one of their most important tasks.

Lenin
Lenin came from nobility and believed in God, and practiced the orthodox religion. When he was 16 years old, he overheard an orthodox priest talking with his father about him. The priest said: "whip him, whip him if he does not obey". This brought Lenin into communism, atheism and out of Christianity.

Lenin became known as the strategist and tactician behind the October revolution in Russia 1917. Lenin used the opium picture in a different way than Marx.

Religion is "The peoples opium", said Marx
Religion is "Opium for the people", said Lenin.

God deniers.

We see that the founder of the theoretical, communistic manifesto, and the first leader of Soviet-union, were both denying God. They denied and cursed a God they knew both lived and is The Creator of this world. By reading more of these men's biographies, I see clearly that they were led over to Satan and the demons areas and captivity. They did not know it themselves, it is one of Satan's tricks – to think that the thoughts comes from one self. If we are not WITH God, then we will automatic be AGAINST. There is no in between.

The Bible says in Matthew.12, 30-31.
"Whoever is not with me is against me, and whoever does not gather with me scatters. Therefore I tell you, every sin and blasphemy will be forgiven people, but the

blasphemy against the Spirit will not be forgiven.

Communism – A Satanic attack of dimensions.

Communism was therefore a satanic attack of dimensions towards this world, through his 2 mediums that he used. First Karl Marx with the communistic manifesto, which was written by Karl Marx and Friedrich Engels in an intimate cooperation. It was released in 1848. Lenin became the one who performed the message. And then history shows others who followed in their footsteps.

It is not hard to see Satan and the demons behind the politics.

We humans are spirit creatures, and in the spirit world there are only 2 actors. It is The Creator Yahweh and the created Satan with the demons. Therefore it is the thoughts of one of these we accept and live out. If it's not God we see shine through the politics of communism, then it is Satan. The important thing is to know our enemy, so we know how to take blessings and curses.

Blessing and curse.
What I see characterize Engels and Karl
Marx communistic manifesto is: They saw
that Christianity and blessing gave growth
and created a difference between believers
and nonbelievers. The nonbelievers did not
get a blessing, but however curse and no
growth. It created a difference between
nonbelievers and believers.

Literature
Kommunisme og religion I sovjet samveldet
- Land og kirke forlag.
Marx Satanist? - Diane Books U.S
Hvorfor er jeg revolusjonær? - Richard
Wurmbrand, Glendale, California91209,
U.S.A.

Chapter 6

Satan and the demons frontal attack on the Christian west.

Religions.
It is man seeking after a god, and again how man thinks god is and how they wish him to be. It is not what God thinks about man, His creation, and that God seeks man, His creation in Christ Jesus His Son. Religion has only one gigantic opponent – and that is Christianity. If we live in a condition that we got our own thought out ideas about who and what god is, then pantheism is a religion.

Pantheism.
Is means seeking after god. It imagines that the divine is everywhere, that God, nature and man in reality is one. Pantheism seeks after God and finds God in everything.

Christianity.
Is God seeking after man through His Son Jesus Christ. Man seeking after God, is and will be a complicated affair, which won't bring us closer to any contact with our God and Creator. Everything God does is simple. It is He who seeks us through His Son Jesus

Christ, whit foundation in Gods Son's
reconciliation on Calvary for all mankind.
This is fantastic, it is simple and it is for
everyone.

New Age thinking.
Listen to this New Age slogan: "The only
way goes inwards".
The Christians had in the 70's a slogan: "One
way". This slogan was about in the same
time as the New Age came with theirs. It is
not hard to see that Satan sticks so close he
can get to Christianity, all the way, in
absolute everything.

The so called New Age thinking.
With its many forms of beliefs has made its
inroad, and we stand up against a remarkable
mix of occultism, cosmic humanism,
mediums, evocation, witchcraft, shamanism,
astrology, tarot cards, different types of
looking into the future, after death
experience, out of body travel, UFO contact,
and elements of Hinduism and Buddhism –
influence of reincarnation belief just
increases.

Astrology is also present.

Get "The stray dog" out -

It was in South California New Age started.

All of this becomes alternatives to the Christian faith. New Age wishes to become an umbrella to most of what exists of new-religiosity.

It was in South California New Age started to take form in few groups during the 50's. It was also here that the New Age movement's premier ideologist, David Spangler, moved and picked up the original ideas and vibes.

David Spangler.

(Much of this is from Google.com and Wikipedia.com)

David Spangler, born 7th of January 1945 in Ohio, is an American clairvoyant and "spiritual" philosopher, who has been one of the founding figures in the New Age movement's ideology.

His first "spiritual" experience in contact with the spiritual, was as a young kid in a car ride with his parents, he was in the backseat. He was looking out the back window when it happened. He got taken outside in the spirit and got a lot of information and experiences. We can see that other occult leaders have had similar experiences. (This will be described more later). When he got back into the car, the vehicle had barely moved.

He has been associated with Findhorn in Scotland, and lived there from 1970 to 1973. Here he wrote the pamphlet: Revelation, the birth of New Age. It became a manifesto for Findhorn and has been called the New Age Bible.

Spangler dated New Age to be contemporary with him, and determined that this new age comes from both outer cosmic powers and change to the inner consciousness.

In this cosmic vision Christ gets a central place. Spangler doesn't envision Christ as a person and salvation figure, but as a cosmic power. Already then did the pioneer group look forward to **"a new age"** .

At the end of his youth he got requests from metaphysical student groups to hold lectures about his own inner contacts, And in 1964, He gave a lecture about "youth and New Age" at a national spiritual conference. This led him to get loads of invitations from all kinds of spiritual and metaphysical organizations across the USA. At that time he did not want to hold lectures, so he said no to all the invitations to concentrate on his

Get "The stray dog" out -

science studies. The year after, in 1965, he felt lead by his own inner spirit to leave college and started to share his own special insight and inner understanding.

This lead him to Los Angeles the same year, and he held many lectures that again lead to many invitations, and resulted in the career he has followed since that time. He was an often used lecturer about spirituality.

In the years that followed Spangler has continued to hold lectures and teach. He has also written quite a few books about spirituality. He is known as the founder of the modern "New Age – Phenomenon".

There were accusations that Spangler had said: Nobody would go into New Age unless he or she makes a way to worship Lucifer and takes a Luciferian initiation. This has been denied and stated that it is false accusations. It is said that others have made this up and that it has wrongly been tied to Spangler. This has been debunked in Spanglers book " Reimagination of the world". Spangler tells us that Lucifer is goanna give us the final Luciferian initiation. That is initiation to New Age. He says that Christ is the same power as Lucifer, and that Lucifer prepares people for an experience of

Christ. Lucifer works inside all of us, to bring us to wholeness as we move into New Age. Spangler teaches that "Lucifer is an agent for God's love". He believes that Lucifer is the angel of man's inner evolution that the light that shows the way to Christ comes from Lucifer... The great initiator. That Lucifer will give us the final initiation that many people in the days to come will face. This is initiation to New Age. Spangler has often been "misunderstood" as a chandler in New Age. That is partly to be blamed on "the transfers" people received when they lived at Findhorn on the Scottish east coast in 1970. Which became the core of his first book "Revelation: The birth of a New Age". It was also founded a similar place in California with the name "Loraine foundation".

Spangler's ideas at that time was the transition between the earlier theosophical esotericism, represented by Alice Bailey and a growing world view which is more postmodern and less metaphysical than theosophical. Spangler himself reported that it took him a few years to develop a language that would communicate clearly and give insight to experiences he has had since childhood. (Google.com)

The phenomenon Esalen Institute.
Already in the 60's another hotbed appeared further north on the same coast. The hotbed laid in the middle of a paradise on earth. If we drive from Santa Barbara, north on Pacific Highway, towards Big Sur and Monterey Bay. We will come to **Hot springs**, by Big Sur. This is the place were hot springs breaks through the earth. The name is **Esalen institute**, one of the most important sources to the New Age – movement – with volcanic heat.

The phenomenon Esalen originated in a warm Christian home in Hamburg 100 years ago.
Covering all the walls are pictures with "Bible words"
The hot "Summer of love" 1967, when the hippies came to this famous region of freedom. It was young people on every spot big enough for a tent. A big number of people came and took part in courses, courses in everything from health to shamanism, one and only for sake of health and their personal development. Either it be shamanism, eastern religiosity or Christian mystic. They take only what stimulates their

emotional development and their physical wellbeing.
Unfortunately it can be observed how these people over time developed immunity against real spiritual impact. It is because of all the Satanic and demonic bindings they get, by participating in all kinds of courses were the occult is in the driver seat.
Esalen is a greenhouse were religions from east and west are planted and grows side by side. Here they are then asked the pragmatic question – does it work? Yes, it works and it is Satanic and demonic, either you feel or understand it, or not.

Esalen Institute, unite "the eternal philosophy" from east and west.
In the 60's, the Esalen institute wanted to unite "the eternal philosophy" from east and west, with new forms of therapy to an eruption which got the pressure waves to roll through the world. The synthesis of spirituality which came from California and got a centre in Esalen, is still influencing what is found in the bookstore shelves and what is written in the culture pages of newspapers.
It is still talked about and written about "The eternal philosophy", and it still gains

Get "The stray dog" out -

ground – The thought that it still exist a common spiritual reality beyond every big religion.

Still it was not until the 80's that New Age became big enough for the global media and got everyone's attention. Bodhi Tree in Los Angeles is one of the world's largest New Age book dealers. The movie actress Shirley Maclaine in Hollywood, became one of the big poster women in the New Age movement, even tho she were not accepted by all there. She also went deep into Spiritism.

In 1970 David Spangler and the 37 years older Myrtle Glines, visited a female therapist in Europe, Findhorn, Scotland to be exact. This became the most important New Age centre on this side of the Atlantic. People came to Findhorn from all the corners of the earth.

Humans are seeking the spiritual at all times, no matter what. We as born again Christians have to be ready at all times. We must continually live in victory in The Spirit, so that It can be spread out of us in victory at all times. The Gospel is a power from God for all eternity. (Rom. 1,16)

You might think its fearful things I am
writing about. Yes, it is – and it is real! As
born again Christians (Not religious) it is a
necessity for us more than anything, to get
an understanding about all the things that
you read about here. These are truths that
Satan has hindered the born again to get an
understanding of. It is of utmost importance
for us to get knowledge about the lies
leading astray, so that we know where to set
in the spiritual blows from The Lord.

Rom. 11, 25 Paul says: "I do not want you to
be unaware of this mystery, brothers"

The Bible got loads of secrets that God
wants to reveal to us. This is also a secret. I
want to show you these things, so that we
can prepare and be ready to attack as soldiers
in Gods army.

Chapter 7.

New Age and spiritism.

We can clearly see the seeking of the spiritual, but which goes completely in the wrong direction. Instead of seeking Christ Jesus, the seeking goes right enough in a spiritual direction, but in a wrong spiritual direction. It is sought spiritual contact with the deceased by mediums, through channelling.

This is something that is impossible! What happens when you seek a person through a medium, is that demons will pretend to be the persons that is tried contacted. What happens then, is that the person seeking will get bound by the demons.

Spiritisms foundation for parapsychology.

Spiritism bloomed up in the last half of the 18th century. In 1882 a group of leading scientists formed a group called "Society for psychical research" in London. With the goal to study spiritism and similar areas, in a critical and scientifically (sense scientifically) way. A society much like them was founded in USA in the year 1888, with the philosopher William James as one of the founders.

Parapsychology didn't become a university subject until 1930's, Then a research laboratory was established at Duke University in Durham, USA, under the lead of J.B Rhine, since then teaching positions in parapsychology has been established in universities, like in Utrecht and Edinburgh. The enormous research activity in among others USA and Soviet-union since the 60's, has given parapsychology "a substantial scientific source material" (scientific sense science).

Parapsychology means: Scientific research of paranormal (earlier called supernatural) phenomenon's. Including the so called ESP (Extra-Sensory-Perception). Phenomenon's as telepathy or transfer of thoughts, Clairvoyance, precognition or the understanding of future events.
As we can understand, spiritism is a concept with ramifications in all sorts and kinds of the supernatural. It is also this that is behind the nature religions, were the animism is a part, and the other religions that are conscious about the supernatural. That is to say that all who start to seek after spiritual and supernatural contact, will get it. They

will get in contact with what science has
called spiritism.

Different kinds of spiritism is the result of
the curiosity of sense knowledge, and the
need for something more than what we can
sense and what is "natural". It is the non-
Christian, not born again human that has
tried to seek out a world outside our "natural
earthly world"

Of course you will get contact with that
world if you seek it out. There are made
attempts to get insight, but that is impossible
for a person that is not born again. The only
thing you can achieve is to see the result of a
spiritual activity. And the different results of
the spiritual activities has then been
catalogued and made into science.

Listen to what Paul clearly said to the church
in 1. Corinth 2, 9-14

"But, as it is written, "What no eye has seen,
nor ear heard, nor the heart of man imagined,
what God has prepared for those who love
him" these things God has revealed to us
through the Spirit. For the Spirit searches
everything, even the depths of God. For who
knows a person's thoughts except the spirit
of that person, which is in him? So also no
one comprehends the thoughts of God except

the Spirit of God. Now we have received not
the spirit of the world, but the Spirit who is
from God, that we might understand the
things freely given us by God. And we
impart this in words not taught by human
wisdom but taught by the Spirit, interpreting
spiritual truths to those who are spiritual.
The natural person does not accept the things
of the Spirit of God, for they are folly to him,
and he is not able to understand them
because they are spiritually discerned.

Here it is talk about getting spiritual insight,
an insight which is available only to those
who are born again. A personality, a soul, a
psyche has no chance to get insight here. The
only thing they can achieve is to see without
understanding a spiritual activity. By
curiosity and engagement to the spiritual,
they can become captured by it and in the
end possessed.
We can draw one thing from what we have
talked about here and that is, that all this are
demonic activities. Satan and his demons are
on the earth with one thing in mind.

In John. 10, 10 it says:
"The thief, the devil, comes only to steal, kill
and destroy".

Get "The stray dog" out -

What's fantastic for mankind is that the devil and all his demons has been defeated once and for all, by the precious Blood of Jesus Christ!

Col. 2, 15. "He disarmed the rulers and authorities and put them to open shame, by TRIUMPHING over them on the cross".

1. John 3, 8 says: " The reason the Son of God appeared was to destroy the works of the devil."

The human has tried to find out things in a world outside the physical world, through a non-Christian condition, a not born again condition. The only thing they will achieve is to make things difficult for themselves. They will only get manipulated by the devils lies. Everything starts by getting repressed by the devil, before you get bound in your soul, personality and in the end you can become possessed.
As born again humans, cleansed of our sins by The Blood of Jesus, we have been freed from the snares of the devil. We can live free from them, and as the only types of humans on the earth we have VICTORY over the devil and all his demons in JESUS NAME.

All outer activities by the demons and the names those activities has been given, is not of any interest. We go directly to the core and take AUTHORITY over the demon, which have already been defeated, no matter what they may say. **We got to go to the origin to the activity, and not to the activity.**
It is victory in Jesus Name!

Spiritism and its history.
Spiritism (english of spiritus), The belief that some humans, so called mediums, got the ability to get in contact with the spirits of the dead, deliver their message, and by their help call forth phenomenon's that can't be explained on the bases of the natural laws that we know. This is very tragic, people move consciously into a spiritual world and they have no clue what they will encounter. Beliefs has been known for ages and are still pretty common among the nature religions. (see chapter Nature religions).
The foundation for modern spiritism can be traced back to the 17th century, to the Swedish nature philosopher and theosophist Emanuel Swedenborg. The modern western, spiritualist movement stated in the town of Hydesville in USA in the year 1848, in

Get "The stray dog" out

connection to some knocking sounds, that some claimed came from spirits.

The spiritualist movement got great propagation also in intellectual societies, and got spread to other countries.

Spiritualist societies and companies with own churches were founded all over the world. The foundation for this faith was the belief that the human spirit continues the life after death, but on a higher level, were they continue to develop and be purified. And that they from this state continues to help the ones that are still living, and that they optionally gets incarnated to new lives on earth.

Spiritism got strong elements from Native American and African origins. (Which then are nature religion). In every dealings with the occult, we will see Satan and the demons in activity, but in different types of tasks.

Theosophy. (Of theo and Greek wisdom) Religious belief that builds on nature mysticism and that God exists in all things. In 1875, Helene Petronova Blavatsky (1831-91) founded a society in USA by the name of Theosophical Society. The goal was to spread a teaching she had written down, a mix of Indian, Egyptian and European traditions.

Prominent in this teaching, is gradually development of mankind through reincarnation (as Hinduism), and the belief in a universal intelligence which is being managed by the so called <u>mahatmas</u>, unworldly masters which teaches the humans.

Helena Petronova Blavatsky became also an important piece for the New Age movement with her teachings.

Annie Besant (1847-1933) became leader of the society after Helena Blavatsky's death. She was also one of the leaders in the Indian congress party (Indian National Congress). The Theosophists got great influence in India. They were often negative towards Christianity.

Antropologie

Spiritual belief crafted a German named Rudolf Steiner (1861-1925). He claimed that the human could through meditation, develop its spiritual abilities to recognize a world beyond senses, and get insight to its own being and cosmic powers that are withheld from nature scientific research.

The movement was founded in 1913, when Steiner broke with theosophy and founded anthroposophy society. Anthroposophy got many followers in many countries, with centre in the free college of spiritual science, Getheanum in Domach Switzerland. There have been founded schools (Steiner-schools) built on the anthroposophy's pedagogic ideas in a number of countries, among them Norway. Steiner developed his own ideas within agriculture, so called biodynamic agriculture, medicine, work with mentally handicapped, art and architecture with more.

Philosophy. (Of Philo and Greek wisdom) Science that wants to find the foundational principles and the context of the existence. The word Philosophy is actually a designation for the love of wisdom.
Originally the designation was used to some extent about all science, partly in the meaning of the teaching of "the true" reality, as the origin of all things.
Gradually the different subjects in science got divided, first to mathematics, astronomy, physics and biology. And then subjects as psychology and sociology.
This made the philosophy loose its former encompassing character. The word

philosophy in daily talk, has no clear demarcated meaning. Philosophy includes metaphysical speculations, questions of spirituality, the origin of knowledge, nature, religion, the foundation and meaning of the art and morale. The five main directions of philosophy is: Logic, epistemology, ethics, aesthetics and metaphysics.

I could have written more about these things, but I would recommend that you, yourself look this up in sources. Then you will find how these things are weaved into the global structure of our society.

It is wee easy to spot how spiritism, Hinduism, New Age and all other spiritual directions seek after the answer to something.

It is only one that is the answer, and that is Jesus Christ Gods living Son. He is the only one that can get mankind into a right life in the spirit world. All other options are controlled and manipulated by Satan and the demons. Without Christ, the Satanic and demonic world will be "controlling" us.

Now I have given you a brief introduction to these things, which in turn will make it easier to understand and live in victory in the areas of the spirit. We are at war in the spirit,

Get "The stray dog" out -

the victory is ours, but we have to understand it, live it and practice it.

Get "The stray dog" out -

Chapter 8.

Santa Barbara in California became mecca for the hippie culture, and one of the centres for New Age ideas.
In Santa Barbara lies the University of California, with world leading scientists when it comes to the New Age movement. It was first in the 70's that the mass media and academic researchers discovered New Age – The wide flow in the ocean of people that did not have its origin in the Jewish Christian heritage.
In reality there were 2 "rivers" that had become one, proven by Gordon Melton and his scientists. **One of "the rivers"** has its headwater way back in occult and metaphysical movements and traditions. And inside these are the west's esoteric knowledge together with the east's religions and perception of life.

When the hippie wave faded.
When the hippie wave faded and its counter culture ebbed out, many people continued their spiritual seeking. It is from this devoted generation amongst other, that the New Age societies recruited their new followers. At the same time "gurus" and meditation

teachers are springing from Asia and across the USA, and pulled the hippies towards themselves. Many exchange the narcotics for meditation and other different kinds of "spiritual" techniques which gives a similar "kick" and intensive experiences.

The other "river"
Builds on the book of Aldous Huxley, writer and professor at the University of California in Santa Barbara. Already in 1945 did he come out with the book "The eternal philosophy".

Esalen institute becomes a legendary "house of growth"
It is now Esalen Institute becomes a legendary "house of growth" were you "graft" these bearing ideas together with new, effective forms of therapy and personal development.
Does it give meaning to use the term New Age about these shifting and wide streams, which have so many different sources? As I see it, it doesn't matter. Because it all is originated and is controlled by the demonic world.

Jesus revival.
Several pop stars at that time joined in and
wrote songs that became hits. Songs that in
many ways became a part of this New Age
movement. Everybody remembers the song
"Let's go to San Francisco, and wear some
flowers in your hear". It was made much
romance and dreams about this time period,
but then the hippie wave ebbed out.
Then they sat there on the beaches in
California. In between bear cans, syringes
and guitars. Then it happened: Jesus from
Nazareth came into their lives and found a
soundboard in this lost, but devoted
generation!
There it was born a song and a people, which
even got into some of our northern
cathedrals in the 70's, and gave us a scent of
the original Christianity – both from
California and Galilee.
In 1973, the year I got saved, waves from the
Jesus revival in California hit our beaches
and the "Jesus revival" started.
**One thing is to experience the emotional
glory in Christ, but we have to get into the
life and the understanding of a life in
victory in the Spirit. It is here the strength
of the Christian shall be shown in Love**

and humility. It is this that I want to lead
you into in this book.

The problem of going away from the denoting "New Age"

Is that there for the time being doesn't exist
any expressions which covers all the aspects
with this movement.

If we for an example said "metaphysical
movement" instead of "New Age", we
would leave out meaningful parts of the
holistic entirety movement – parts which
don't consider themselves as "metaphysical",
but still are a part of New Age, or formerly
meant they were.

"Metaphysics" includes also certain religious
sects, such as Christian Science, which
doesn't fit into the New Age categories.

"I really want to know", said Harry Månsus,
(writer of the book "The cosmic cathedral")
"What were the life visions that existed
behind those quenched eyes. But I dear not
go over to them and ask. Are you shadows
from a faded heyday? Are you surviving
"pilgrims" of the people which once invaded
these beaches with their guitars, drugs and
dreams about a new age?"

Get "The stray dog" out –

One can clearly see that there are no spiritual understanding here, they are way out on a side-track of the truth.
Jesus Christ and His reconciliation on Calvary has been long forgotten. And not to mention Jesus Christ's victorious blood, over all the works of Satan and the demons.
Physics is the physical, like the the world we live in.
Metaphysics is to New Age a spiritual thing, something outside the physical. If you seek into this, you are a victim for the demons in a blink of an eye, no matter if you understand it or not.

Christen Jesus.
In the centre stood Jesus Christ, or as they called it: **Christen Jesus.**
Occult speakers gave out their speeches in the gatherings and enticed the people. New Age wanted to be a gathering of religions. The inner Christ goes as a red tread through the new-religious movement. **It is important according to the new religions to distinguish between "Jesus and Christ".**
These terms have 2 completely different meanings according to them.
One of the theosophist pioneers said: "The Churches biggest mistake is to identify

Christ with Jesus. Jesus was a historical
prominent person, while Christ is a state of
mind, namely to experience unity with the
eternal divine principle. Everyone who
prepares for this, can experience divine
principle.
Jesus experienced "The inner Christ". So did
also Buddha and all other great religious
masters. You can call this inner
enlightenment "Christhood", "Buddhahood",
"Krishna consciousness" or whatever you
want. The reality you experience, is in every
occurrences exactly the same; your unity
with the universal "Christ-self".
"Therefor can every human that are good,
find Christ in his inner being... Be he Jewish,
Hindu or Christian." Blavatsky 1892-84)
"Christ mass incarnation has already started,
the cosmic Christ power. This is the very
sign of "the Age of Aquarius". The result
will be a new mankind on the new earth."
(Spangler 1976; 133)
One of Spanglers closest co-workers, George
Travelyn, says in his book "Vision of the
aquarion age", that the mission of Christ is to
bring under control the two disturbing
spiritual powers. "Lucifer" (The fallen spirit,
originally light bringer) and "Ahriman"(a

Get "The stray dog" out -

Persian word for an eternal disturbing spirit, much used by Steiner.)

It is specified that the demonic powers are not evil in themselves. They shall also be saved at one time. "The evil" is the fact that these powers are out of control. The creator of this Jesus-avatar-idea in the west, Swami Vinekananda, combined this understanding with a powerful attack on the traditional Christianity. **There is no "only begotten Son" of God.**

The Gospel is a power of God. (Rom.1, 16) Do you understand this? THE GOSPEL is a POWER of God! The world's Christians are whizzing around in a religiosity that they themselves are not aware of. Satan laughs at it all! Speaking in tongues and "faith" and all the biblical things in the world won't help, if you don't throw yourself in it, and challenge Satan and the demons, and bring home the victory! If you don't do this, then please be silent instead.

Believe it, do it and live it – The Gospel which is a power of God, so that Satan and the demons will know who are in the lead in Jesus Name. If we don't bring home the already perfect victory in Jesus Name – Then Satan will continue to have victories. He can give you more troubles than you are able to understand. This he will continue to do to mankind until he is thrown into the lake of fire for all eternity. (Revelation 20, 10) Yes, for eternity! It sounds good, but it is a long wait. Until then, we have to stand up and defeat Satan and the demons on all fields.

Get "The stray dog" out .

Chapter 9.

Recipe for New Age.
2 cups hope (The fear is carefully sifted out)
2 cups change of the consciousness (add
Yoga, narcotics or meditation to taste)
3 tablespoon self-consciousness,
assertiveness, self-respect (be careful to melt
away all sceptical thoughts)
1 topped teaspoon peace
1 big piece of love
1 pinch of humanism, eastern mysticism and
occultism
1 hand full piety
1 measure experience with mysticism

Mix it all together and cook it carefully in a
friendly environment. Add your most
appealing dreams, mixed with positive
thinking and good vibes.

False teachers.
Every false teaching is complicated, yeah
rich in detail, so that you can never get a full
understanding. You grab hold of small
things, accept it and take for granted that the
rest is in order. No matter what, it is going
astray.

Get "The stray dog" out -

It is interesting to see how close to the truth, Gods Word, The Bible it all is! They have included Jesus Christ God's living Son, but not in His fullness!
He is never pictured in a way that shows Him as the Saviour of the world. That, you will never find!
The Gospel of Jesus Christ, Gods living Son, is really simple to understand. Then it is also the eternal Truth.

We are created by God Jehovah, Yahweh.
Mankind is in being godlike, because we are created by God. We are created to live in God's presence!
People try with different "spiritual" techniques, with mystical experiences like yoga, meditation, magic rituals and other stuff, to get spiritual power. In these ways they become initiated, literally becoming the creator – they think. Not by becoming united with God, but by creating their own reality, by the strength it is to master your own mind.
This state is "enlightenment" or "salvation", and leads to reincarnation. Or that the wheel of death or reincarnation will stop.

The arrival of the Guru and demons.
I remember the guru Maharishi Mahesh
Yogi, from India, which is the founder of the
Transcendental meditation movement. I
remember well the times he came to
Norway.
He tried to present a modern angel to
reincarnation.
It had gotten the western inclination to
selective confession when he said: "**We
must bring our message to the West, to
those who have a habit to rush and take
things lightly.**"
He came in his Indian guru dress with his
long beard. He arranged courses for
entrepreneurs. Some young people came,
they were Western with suits and nice short
hair. He presented his meditation techniques
with meditation, focus, concentration, yoga
and more.
There were also testimonies by students who
had gotten improvement on their
performance at school, after they had started
practicing Transcendental meditation.
**Transcendental meditation is in a nut
shell: Find peace and God without the
only bridge to God, namely Jesus Christ.**
This opens up the mind for demonic ideas,
which in time can lead to the destruction of a

human. This is an astonishing mix of mystic and the occult, the backdrop is completely demonic. It can of course not be seen until the bindings are in place.

Another reason for reincarnation thinking.
One of the reasons reincarnation thinking got such a great appeal in the West, is connected to the religious New Age-movement, and their "profit", like Erhard Seminars Training, Yoga, Zen and the occult counterculture belief that we are entering the astrological golden age.

The age of the waterman, Aquarius.
The Age of Aquarius is central term within New Age. I will mention some of this, even if it has no root in reality, it is something Satan and the demons are using to seduce mankind. We shall not be ignorant about anything, The Lord wants us to have a spiritual overview, and this is something we all can get.
Hypnotherapist Dr. Helen Wamback from California, is a spokeswoman for the New Age thinking. She have specialized in getting people to remember claimed past lives under hypnosis.

Those hypnotized would all let themselves
be reincarnated back to this time, which is
the Age of Aquarius, because it is a new age.
In this period there were several that took
LSD to open their minds and get back in
time, which you could supposedly do under
hypnosis. Several people from that time,
after experiencing LSD and other narcotics,
got committed to mental hospitals and stayed
there. All this happened during the hippie
period.
Inside the popular culture of the New Age,
there is a common understanding about the
Age of Aquarius, that it will bring an
extensive new spirituality, were you seek
inwards yourself, and react by intuition,
rather than external rules. The term is also
known from the movie/musical Hair (1967).

The Age of Aquarius.
Is a central term within New Age, the term
comes from astrology, there it describes in
what sign the spring equinox will occur.
Equinox changes star signs in intervals of
2100 years.

The earth has been in the sign of the fishes
since the antiquity. And this shall last a
couple hundred years more, until the sun gets

into the sign of Aquarius. Several dates have been given, by different astrologers, to date the change: 2150, 2654 and more.

Other people claim the change has already happened, and ties it to events in history, in 1433 or 1844. Some astrologers thinks that the change from one age in astrology to another will bring with it paradigm changes to religion and science. Other astrologers says that the Age of Aquarius began in 2012.

The change is not just a passing and a change of time in the astrology perspective. It is a radical change of the world and mankind. We will get an epoch, with a new and different life quality for the existence as human. A term that is often used is **transformation.** (I have gotten this information from some scientific articles on Google.com).

According to the New Age thinking. "The age of Aquarius" will bring a new spiritual revolution, a new consciousness and a new type of religiosity.

The hippies and Slotts park.

This shows were the world is in the spiritual picture, it is totally seduced and deceived by Satan and the demons. Christ is the only answer in all things. This might sound very easy, but it is the pure truth and can be experienced by everyone that wants to experience it.

I remember the time well, Slotts park in Oslo which became the hangout for the hippies. Drugs started to flow there. One of my friends who was a good athlete, died of an overdose there in Slotts park.

Everything was just "love", that's what people talked about. But reality was something different. "Make peace, not war" was the slogan back then. Hair the musical came to Oslo, this I remember very well. I was a little into the theatre- and film milieu, and was there during the premier show of the "Hair-musical", with actors and singers which came from London.

Above the stage all the lights and scenes were tied up. And around that a footbridge. I laid there on the footbridge and looked down onto the heads of the actors and watched the premier. This was about 5 years before I got

Get "The stray dog" out -

saved. The Age of Aquarius which became so popular at that time, fell pretty quick. It was a fallen star. We also know about someone else that was a fallen star, Satan which back then was named Lucifer, angel of light.

It smells " Spiritism dressed in Hinduism" of it all. I sensed that something was not right, already at the premier, this was in 1968. I was not yet been saved. After I got saved I started to understand the spiritual negative in this.
No matter what comes and goes of spiritual varieties outside Christ, is from Satan. All spiritual that does not confess Christ Jesus as Lord. Is of Satan!

You will never get an opponent of the Gospel of Jesus Christ, which is involved in the spiritual, to confess Jesus Christ as Lord! It is completely impossible. So here we have a secure test. It is written in

1 Corinth 12,3 Paul says: "No one can say Jesus is Lord except in The Holy Spirit."

Fantastic, what a confession, what a proclamation, what a test and what a revealing of lies and the truth!

Hindu festivals.
I have been to many Hindu festivals in India through the years. People that torment themselves are protected under the god Shiva. Ascetics torment themselves voluntary, some hang in the air by big hooks through the skin of their back and legs, other walk around for days with hooks through their tongues or in more private parts. Others were laying on rusty nail beds or barbed wire, others again let themselves be flogged until the blood flows. One ascetic had been standing for 38 years, without laying or sitting down once, much of the time he stood in water. Some cut off different parts of the body, or touched red glowing iron. Withstand sufferings, hunger, longing and more.
In the demonic pressure and atmosphere, with possession of demons, this goes on for days, while ascetics does this often their whole life.
A worshiper of Shiva lies on a gnarled wooden board, with his fingertips pressed hard into his cheeks. He has not moved his

hands for a long long time. Other people feed him and cares for him. He lies under the shade from a tree in on the Shiva temples courtyards.

The nails on his fingers has grown into his cheeks. Other followers of Shiva has put flowers around his ghastly dirty hair, and his forehead is painted with some wide white stripes. If you come in contact with the ascetic, he will say: "I seek nothing anymore, I myself has become god."

There are also made human sacrifices to the Hindu god kali. Kali demands sacrifices of blood. I remember the first time I was at a Hindu festival in India. I spoke the Word of God from an altar of sacrifice, thousands of people were present. Later on, someone told me that children had been sacrificed at the very same festival, it was also in the newspapers. Human sacrifice has become illegal in India, but it still happens underground.

Rhythmic drumbeats could be heard everywhere non-stop. And one ascetic stood and stared at the sun, this he had done daily for some time, and had gone completely blind.

Krishna is one of many gods in India that are worshiped and in some places highly revered. In relation to this, we must take note, that this god incarnation is one of the most important dogma and doctrines of Hinduism.

At some point I saw some guys from the West that practiced Hare Krishna, They were hitting their braids against each other and yelled; "Hare, Hare, Hare Krishna". They felt so lost, and got terrified of what they saw. No, you don't play with Satan and the demons!

The deceit of Satan and the demons.
The youth of the West understood the western version of Hinduism as something romantic and exciting, it was only peace and love. No and No, it is not like that at all! The West lets itself be deceived with its blue eyes wide open.
We can clearly see the demons infernal attack on the western, Christian world.
The demons had gotten loads of tools to use, that did not get that big appeal to the West as the demons had hoped, but they have gotten a grip.

Get "The stray dog" out

When the Guru came to Oslo.
When the guru Maharishi Mahesh Yogi from India, came to Norway for the first time. He arranged seminars for entrepreneurs in Oslo. I remember he came in his white robe and long grey beard. He wanted us to find ourselves, peace and concentration. He wanted to get inside the West in a wily way, with his belief in reincarnation.
A female guru and a younger man that also were a guru, came to Norway about the same time as Mahesh also wearing white robes. This young man which was born in 1957, stepped into "spiritual maturity" after his father's death (which was a perfected master). Now it was the son's turn, and he came to Oslo. He had millions of followers back in India, see how Satan can seduce people!
After some time we never saw neither of them again, it was not the right conditions for their message to grow in this country. What we did not see, was all the demons that had come along with them, which stayed after they had left.
Hare Krishna never became a big movement in Norway, they had for a period a place of meeting at Frogner in Oslo. It withered away little by little.

Spiritual attack on the nations.
I got as mentioned Christian a while after
these events of demonic attacks, but none
of this got handled or even understood by
the Christians.
And as I have understood, it has never been
taken care of by any Western country.
This was an attack on the West, the
materialistic nations, the Christian nations.
Why have all the Western nations become
rich in the material? It is because of one
reason. It is because these nations got the
Bibles clear message about Jesus Christ
and His reconciliation work as a
foundation. For this reason alone has
Gods promise of Blessing come to the
West.
Then it is also easy to understand why
hunger and natural disasters ravages the
nations without Christ, Nations that live out
all kinds of different religions.

Occultists and spiritualists are spiritually
aware.
The occult world are spiritually conscious
and think they use Satan and the demons, but
it is Satan and the demons that use the
occultists and the spiritualists in their
purposeful work.

Get "The stray dog" out -

Occultists and spiritualists let themselves be used voluntary in Satan and the demons world. Everything starts of as an adventure and an experiment for these people, but ends up in the clutches of Satan and the demons. Then it is no more fun and games.

Most bound – some possessed.
Most people have become bound by demons, while a few have become possessed. The possessed are those that pledge allegiance to Satan and let him become lord in their lives. They that don't do it, are bound by Satan. These type of people you can find in every part of society, in every profession. Be it Doctors, nurses, lawyers, bank or store employees. Yes, they are everywhere.
You will never know when you come in contact with these kind of people, without them telling you anything about their "hidden world", their spirit will still affect you.
Spiritsm has gotten accepted into the modern society, both inside and outside the new religions.
Spiritism is one of the most widespread forms of religions we know. The spirits of those that have passed away, possesses the higher knowledge that humans can take part

in through certain mediums. This is actually the manipulating message of demons.

One should be aware of that spiritism is a natural part of all new-religious movements.

Chapter 10.

Are you as a Christian on the offense or are you a lazy one.
Does the Christians have a task in the world today? Does the Christians have a task which has to be carried out with insight and authority?
If you are a Christian on the offense, you will always register demonic activity with your spirit, if it is in your vicinity.
The "lazy" Christians will never notice anything, but rather be walked all over by these spiritual powers.

It is war in the world of the spirit, and it will last until Jesus returns.
Again – the victory is ours, use it.
The world needs the Christian type that are on the offense, those that know who they believe in and live it! Popular Christianity full of "Cheers and worship songs" is not what we need. We need to get out the warriors in Christ, those that STAND after they have CONCURED ALL in Jesus Name. The Name of Jesus Christ must once more be heard every where! With great enthusiasm over His victory for you in your life, and through your life into the world that is

around you. You shall be the house of His power. You are the mission centre, you shall stand before The Lord Jesus ALONE. This is what the Gospel of Jesus Christ really is, the victory of Christ FOR you and IN you. A house is never stronger then the weakest block.

There is no mediator between you and Christ.
The place where the meetings are held, or the pastor you have, is no mediator between you and Christ. It is YOU and JESUS. You can't hide behind anyone, it is only Christ and you. It is to Him you are responsible, no one else!
If you think this sounds too harsh, then the question is: Are you willing to let Christ get full control of your life, to become your Lord? If you are not willing to let Him, then don't throw away more time on the religious life you are living, find something else to do.

Every soldier is trained for war.
If you want to join Gods army, you have to become a warrior. You got to enlist for duty, and submit yourself under the authority of the warrior academy. You have to obey in everything. Your opinion have no say here,

Get "The stray dog" out

but only the authority that is above you. Real tough, yeah, but do you want to become a warrior or not?

If you pass the soldier training of The Lord, then Satan and the demons will be terrified of you. Were ever you go, they will back off!

The provisional government's meeting in Bucharest, Romania.

I sat in meetings in the provisional government of Romania, after the dictator had been removed. It was in the end of December in 1989. I was inside the administration of the nation before any other foreign diplomat came.

The Indian guru woman in Bucharest.

2 days of meetings with the provisional government of Romania, gave the opportunity I needed to get started with evangelizing. After some time we had big meetings on football stadiums, and inside sports facilities. It is wonderful to be part of bringing the power of The Spirit into god denying nations, run by dictators.

An unpredicted challenge appeared. An Indian guru, a woman, had managed to sneak past me. She had rented a hall that could room 5000 people. The hall was full of

people that waited, and the guru woman
showed up in a big fancy car with a private
chauffeur. And along the path from her car
and to the hall there were small lights all the
way.

On stage 50 of her disciples sat in white long
robes. She herself sat on silk cushions in all
the rainbows colours.

Here sat 5000 people that just came out of
the clutches of a dictator and then Satan
comes in from the side-line to tie up the
nation again! I felt in my heart that I could
not allow this to happen.

"Naskut de now" - "Get born again", that
was my first book that got translated to
Romanian. I had already printed 20 000
copies. Terje Westgård, which was my
organizer in Romania, had arranged
Christians to stand by all the exits of the hall.
They had an abundance of the book to hand
out to the followers when they came out.

Kjell Martinsen and I, (a friend of mine, we
started Norsk Nødhjelp together) went inside
and up behind the stage curtain. On stage sat
all the disciples of the guru and her herself
sat on silk cushions. We sat down in the
middle of her disciples on stage, and prayed
to The Lord for further guidance. After a
while we stood up while the woman was

speaking, went over to her and asked to get the microphone. She gave me the mice without saying anything. I asked if anyone in the arena spoke English, I needed an interpreter. A man came up to interpreter and I started preaching to the people.

I proclaimed the Gospel and broke the power of evil. Some of the woman's bodyguards came and carried me outside. I did nothing to resist. The books got handed out, and the victory was won in Jesus Name.

After this I was over the whole nation with big crusades, and multitudes of people came to Christ and miracles happened everywhere. The Indian guru lady did never return to Romania.

Spreading of the Reincarnation-gospel in the west.

The reincarnation-gospel proclaims. "Adam drove the whole world into sin and death. Through different kinds of reincarnations, Adam managed to work his way up to the position of Christ."

Think what kind of seduction and manipulation of the truth!

If you don't make it in this life, then the Western reincarnation-theology gospel says: "No sweat, because you get a chance to come back and improve your position in the next round, until you have finally reached the top – nirvana."

Put an end to the painful circle of reincarnation.
If we ask any Hindu or Buddhist ascetic, which has made a wove to deny the pleasures of this world, and spends his life up in a cold monastery in Himalaya, year in and year out.
"Why do you do this?" Then they would answer without hesitation, what we also could predict "Because I am tired of the purposeless agony in suffering and reincarnation. I want to be free from slavery to karma by mastering spiritual techniques, a strict way of living and meditation. I want this to be my last life." Whatever the case is with entering or leaving the wheel of reincarnation, the goal is to rise up in God or cosmos, or more precisely expressed: To become God, to get an end to reincarnation's painful circle. Reincarnation is closely tied to the Hindu tradition.
We can see that modern followers of reincarnation try to mix eastern and western mind-sets of faith.

They transplant the Hindu and Buddhist mind-set into a cultural heritage that is mostly Christian.
The kind of reincarnation that is hailed by occultists, is the belief that an individual human soul goes through a great number of following reincarnations as a human, relieved by periods in "hidden worlds"... every individual soul is not "created" special, but is begotten from a natural "budding" from a collective soul.
The Buddhist word for heaven, *nirvana* literally means "blown out, quenched". Buddha was very interested in the problem of pain and suffering. He claimed that the source of the dilemma that humans are in, is that the mind and the body are bound to the physical world, or more precisely expressed: bound to existence itself. The logic solution is then to stop existing. To stop being reincarnated, of course. Because of these Buddhist statements, the Buddhism has often been called "The atheistic religion."
The thought of reincarnation has been a main element in the Hindu and Buddhist thinking since long before Christ.

Get "The stray dog" out .

Chapter 11.

The unconscious, but determined attempt to combine the two spiritualties – which is eternally impossible.

Spiritualism.
Both in spiritualism and spiritism the belief of communication with the dead are essential. The spirits are contacted by mediums, which communicate directly with the spirits and convey the messages, guidance, support and teachings.
Spiritualism does not follow any special teachings. Spiritism follows a tenet and teaching which is begotten directly from highly evolved spirits, like Jesus for an example. This teaching involves the philosophy and practice of spiritism and is called the doctrine of spiritism.

The spiritual existence.
Those who are a *trance medium,* is a medium that experience themselves as a hollow pipe. In full trust they lend their bodies to the incorporeal spirits which are called entities, but the Bible calls them demons.

The demons are many, but Satan is one. I write Satan with little s, big s is only at the beginning of a sentence. This is intentional, since I cannot and will not under any circumstance give any exaltation to that name.

Through mediums the demons always present themselves as persons that have lived before, but now live forever after death. Which is not true, since the Bible clearly teaches us that no one can raise from the dead. If we die from the earth life, then the door back to the earth life is closed. This I will get more into later in the book.

The evil spirits manipulations, lies and deceit.

There are people that presents their bodies as mediums for the evil spirits.

The evil spirits are so crafty that they can get people to become mediums without them understanding that the demons are manipulating them!

The demons get the people to think that they got a special gift, which works in such a way that the dead can speak through them. This is not the case at all! The truth is that they are mediums for demons! They get bound by

Get "The stray dog" out -

demons and the demons makes deals with them.

They are completely tied up, with no possibility to become free. The only way for them to become free, is to surrender to Jesus Christ! When they do it, there has to be a Christian helper present, which has the authority to loosen people from the power of the demons.

When a person comes to a trance medium, or the existence (demon). Then they are bound, until optionally the Salvation in Christ happens to them.

John of God, the medium from South America.

John of God is a man from South-America that has been a medium for 50 years. He draws multitudes of people world over. In his meetings in Atlanta, Georgia, USA, 2500 people attended every night. Everywhere he goes, thousands are gathered.

People with physical and mental needs were rushing in.

Without reservation they do everything he tells them to do, and accepts everything he tells them to accept. A lot of people are healed in his meetings, there is no doubt.

The thing that either the medium or the followers are aware of, is that there are demons doing the work. People are voluntary walking into partnership with the entities, which is a demon.
"Divine Love" heals people they say, healing of the spirit is the most important, they emphasize that. The medium presents himself "humble and full of love".

A healer is made.
There are many "healers" in the world, even here in Norway there are several. What you also can notice about "the healers", is that they have many different forms and expressions in their "way of healing".
I want to talk about one "healer" and how he came into it from the beginning. We got to understand how Satan and the demons got long term, and patient plans to get their instruments ready for the task they are getting into.

Chosen.
When it comes to getting into service for the kingdom of God, Then God often chooses the person from a very young age. The same we see happen on Satan and the demons

side. They choose their tools, victims, from an early age.

Into the demonic service.
John of God came into his demonic service already at the age of 9. Then he got a premonition, or as the spiritual gifts call it, "word of knowledge" or Word of wisdom". Satan and the demons will always try to copy everything God does. Satan and the demons cannot under any circumstance create anything of their own. They can only to a certain degree copy what God does, but of course without the power of The Holy Spirit. It is done with Satanic/demonic powers.
John of God grew up in a catholic and spiritist home. As I see it, he never wondered if it were Satan and the demons that revealed themselves through saints for him. He think they are helpers, energies that he is a channel/medium for. He doesn't think further than that. From the Bible we can clearly see that this is the work of Satan and the demons.
Sometime later, John of God felt depressed and was weakened by hunger. He lived in poverty. He then took shelter under a bridge in the outskirts of his town.

The beginning of bondage.
His family had either food, money or work.
He then walked down to the river under the
bridge, then a beautiful lady called out for
him. She told him to come closer.
They spent one afternoon together in
conversation. The next morning he
remembered the young lady's beauty and
mildness, and got drawn down to the river
again for another conversation. He got
amazed when he noticed a shining strip of
light were she had sat down. He got even
more astonished, when she called him by
name.

Bound strongly in the soul/personality.
She said that he should seek out Spiritist
Centre of Christ the Redeemer. So he did,
and met the boss of the centre who said he
had been waiting for him. At the same
moment he passed out.
When he regained consciousness several
hours later, he was surrounded by a large
group of people. They told him that he had
been "incorporated". Now he had become
bound by demons.
They told him that he had been
"incorporated" by the spiritual entity of king
Solomon, and that more than 50 persons had

become healed afterwards, before he came to himself again.

The church were mesmerized by his abilities as medium and "the healing" that had taken place. At this time he was a teenager.

The next few months became an intense period, with spiritual instructions and guidance from the spiritual entity.

Later on he understood that the beautiful lady by the river was the holy Rita Cascias spirit. She had told him: "Love and believe in the higher creation that is god."

Here we see the speech of lie and confusion.

God is not created by anything, he is not a higher creation that is god.

Our God Jehovah, Yahweh is Himself the Creator, and He has created himself. Jehovah means: "The self-existing which reveals himself".

There is no holy Rita Cascias either, it is a revelation from a demon.

As born again humans we must know the scripture, the Bible. And learn to live and walk in the Spirit, and to exercise the ability to test spirits.

This is a necessity now more than ever in history of mankind.

The medium I now speak about, got guidance in many spiritual affairs for the next 5-6 years. He continued with his "healing" every day, as the years passed. He talks about that without the grace of god, nothing of what he does had been possible. And he appears in love. Once every year he gets a new incorporation, (new strong bindings) from the so called "holy Ignatius", which is a demon purporting to be a person. When he has his great gatherings and appears, according to himself as a total "trance medium", he becomes like a hollow pipe.

In full trust he commits his body to the incorporeal spirits which are called entities, which I will call demons, as the Bible says. These spirits have, according to him, been remarkable humans in their physical life on earth.

This form of embodiment they call "incorporation", they then work through him, invisible and visible operations.

It is here in surgery he uses a fruit knife and long scissor with cotton and holy water which he sticks up the nostrils. The entire

fruit knife is shoved up the nostrils, and
blood is pouring out.

Do you see the gravity?

Can you see the importance of whole hearted
Christians, totally surrendered, maturity and
spiritual in The Holy Spirit?
We are in a war in the spirit – the victory has
been won! But we got to get it out – if not
we will lose. What do you want?
This world needs the born again soldiers of
Jesus.

Demons go both ways with sickness.

In the New Testament we see Jesus
commanding the disabling spirit which had
bound the woman, and bent her over so she
could not fully straighten herself for 18
years, we can read that in Luke. 13, 11-13.
Furthermore we can see in Matthew. 9:32-
33. The mute who was possessed and led to
Jesus. When the evil spirit was chased out,
the mute could talk.
Here we see that sickness is demons that
come and occupy people. Furthermore we
see them cast out by Jesus, and Further on by
the followers of Jesus, in Jesus Name. They
are not thrown into perdition, for that time
has not yet come. They are sent back into the

skies, there they are still ready to attack other people.

The medium John of God.
When it comes to the medium John of God, They have an opinion that there are different entities that heals different kinds of diseases. They say that there are one for diabetes, one for heart problems and so on.
The Bible teaches clearly, that demons are carriers of the illnesses they put on people. And just as easy as they put a sickness on a person, they can remove it. So in this way the medium John of God experienced healing.
Friend, we got to grasp the spiritual truths and live them fully. We are the victorious ones, we reveal the tactics of the demons and win every time in Jesus Name!

The demons puts on and takes away sickness.
The reality behind this, is that the demons puts sickness on people to torment them. The demons then works through mediums and takes the sickness off again.
This is not healing, it is just a sickness demon that goes on and off to capture people in his trap.

Get "The stray dog" out

The medium John of God also says, that when a person has gotten help from an entity or demon, the entity will follow that person further through life.
Then the person will for always be bound by that demon.

You experience freedom from sickness for a while.
In Matthew. 12, 43-45 Jesus explains what happens when an unclean spirit, a sickness spirit for body or mind, get cast out from a human. What happens is that, at a time not given, the demon will come back to that person to see if he is "available", after it has been cast out.
If it is available, the Bible says, that Jesus said: "Then it goes and brings with it seven other spirits more evil than itself, and they enter and dwell there, and the last state of that person is worse than the first."

There is not health no matter the cost.
This is my advice for the reader: "There is not health no matter the cost." I understand that people want to live as healthy human beings.

There is almost as many sicknesses as
people. People all over the world suffer
terribly under the torment from sickness.
When an offer of good health comes our
way, then the human will naturally seek that
way in hope of getting well. This the demons
have noticed and they stand ready to
manipulate mankind. Satan will heal and
bind mankind, so that he can get them and
not Jesus Christ.

**The demons rejoice when they torment
humans.**
There is only one right way for mankind and
that is Jesus Christ, God Jehovah's living
Son. And the reconciliation, the victory He
won on Calvary for mankind's freedom in
every area.
It is in Jesus Christ our victory, freedom, joy,
love, harmony, health and our relation with
Him and other people are found. Christ is
our Saviour, our hope, our everything.

It is demons who appear.
So in every spiritist séance, were a "person"
appears through a "medium", it is not the
person that appears, but a demon. They have
the availability in our circumstances and our
lives that they are given. They pretend to be

the person that is sought for. We have an example of this in the Bible.

Let us read in 1.Samuel. 28,7-11:
Then Saul said to his servants, "Seek out for me a woman who is a medium that I may go to her and inquire of her." And his servants said to him, "Behold, there is a medium at En-dor." So Saul disguised himself and put on other garments and went, he and two men with him. And they came to the woman by night. And he said, "Divine for me by a spirit and bring up for me whomever I shall name to you." The woman said to him, "Surely you know what Saul has done, how he has cut off the mediums and the necromancers from the land. Why then are you laying a trap for my life to bring about my death?" But Saul swore to her by the Lord, "As the Lord lives, no punishment shall come upon you for this thing." Then the woman said, "Whom shall I bring up for you?" He said, "Bring up Samuel for me."

This woman from En-Dor, was a necromancer. She was supposedly capable to summon the dead back from death. (Which is impossible). She was a spiritist. She told Saul she had conjured Samuel. **It was not**

Samuel that appeared, but a demon. This demon had knowledge about Samuel and impersonated him.

Here the Bible is crystal clear, people that are dead, cannot come back. We see king Saul in his desperation and confusion seek out the help from demons. In this state of mind people are open for almost anything. Therefore, more than ever, must we the born again believers, stand firm in wisdom and in the power of The Holy Spirit.

Spiritism and its history.

Spiritism (English of spiritus), a belief that some people, so called mediums are able to come in contact with the spirit of the dead, deliver a message from them, and by their help produce phenomenon's that cannot be explained on the basis of the natural laws that we know.

Such belief has been known since the dawn of time, and is still quite common among the nature religions (see chapter nature religion). The foundation for modern spiritism can be traced back to the 17th century, to the Swedish nature philosopher and theosophist Emanuel Swedenborg.

The modern western, spiritist movement occurred in the city of Hydesville in USA in the year 1848, in connection to some knocking sounds, which some believed came from spirits. The spiritist movement got widespread, also in intellectual circles, and across country borders. All over the world spiritist societies and associations with their own churches were founded.

The foundation of it was, that the human spirit continues to live after death on a higher level, Were they continuously evolve and are purified, And that they from there continues to watch the living and try to aid them, and that they might get reincarnated to new earthly lives.

Spiritism got large elements from the Native American and African (which are nature religions).

The death of the spiritist pope.
At the death of the spiritist pope, Chico Xavier's death, there was a procession of 2500 people every hour in front of the coffin. Among the attending were leaders from Brazil and Islamic nations. Jewish and Christian world leaders were also attending.

The world lives in blindness from God
Jehovah's opponent and his co-workers,
Satan and the demons.

The creed of the medium John of God.
He got a creed in what he stands for. It goes
as follows:
"All my life I have been a pious follower of
the holy Rita Cascia.
I have been a catholic since birth.
As a spiritist I have to read and study a lot.
First time I received an incorporation (strong
bindings), was in Campo Grande, in the
Spiritist Centre of Christ the Redeemer.
I do not preach religion.
Do not teach any specific religion.
My belief is universal.
I believe in the creator.
I believe in virgin Mary.
I believe in the disciples.
I believe in the real Freemasons.
I know that God and the compassionate
spirits are with me.
There is an entourage, a group of
compassionate spirits, who works together
from the spiritual realms.
I believe in Jesus. (Which Jesus? Not The
Saviour!)

Get "The stray dog" out .

I believe in god, because he is my father.
(But which god?)
I am raised catholic and spiritist. The family
is tipping more towards spiritism.
After having met Chico Xavier, which I call
the spiritist pope, I cannot even call myself a
spiritist."

John of Gods wife Ana says:
"My family are partially catholics and
partially spiritists. I experience an
unconditional love when I am with the
entities (The demons). It is only god that
heals (her god)."

Get "The stray dog" out -

Chapter 12

Satan builds a network across the world.
Here we see that he first got contacted by the demons, to get the binding started. To further get so heavily bound by demons that you can possible be. Several shamans have followed in his footsteps, they have bowed down to him both physical and spiritual, and has been taken by the same demons.

The same is with his wife Ana. These reach millions of people. Those that follow them are from all working classes. They affect everyone, every day, everything around them.

They that receive help from the entities through the medium, must go into partnership with the entity. Here we can clearly see that the demons won't let go of you. Here we need exorcism, by the help of a human filled with The Holy Spirit's power in their life.

"Altar call of Satan".
What I can clearly see sticking out, is something I will call "Satan's altar call". Satan call people to himself in different ways.

Some by letting them see him as he truly is. These are people that take a conscious stand

for Satan, and let him become lord of their
life. These are the ones that becomes
worshipers of Satan, they become possessed
in their spirit.
Others gets into different religions and
lifestyles, without them knowing that Satan
is behind it. They believe they only
experience spirituality. The truth is that these
people get bound by demons in their
soul/personality.
Further we got those who become mediums,
channels for demons, entities. They also
don't know that they are working with Satan
and the demons. They talk about spirituality,
energies, saints and god. They also become
bound in their soul/personality.
Satan's and the demons spirit's presence is
fascinating, attractive and binding.

It is exactly as the Bible says in John.10, 10
:"Satan, The Thief, comes only to steal
murder and destroy".

Further the Bible says in John. 8, 44 :" Satan
is a lier, and the father of lies".

**People accept "Satan's altar call" and
they let all the different alternatives
become their lives leaders.**

Get "The stray dog" out -

- Satan and the demons presents "almost everything", and people swallow the bait.
- He can present god, but what god? Not God Jehovah!
- He can present Jesus, but not Jesus Christ God Jehovah Yahweh's living Son!
- He can present the cross, but not that Jesus Christ is Jehovah Yahweh's living son.
- He talks about love and mercy, but not according to the Bibles clear teaching.

- Satan does of course try to use "love and grace" as a shield, to prevent attacks.
- It is never mentioned at all, that Christ lived His life here on earth without sinning even once, and that He then gave His life for the sins of man and conquered Satan for all eternity on Calvary cross.
- To then bring back to God, God's own blood which was in the veins of Jesus, without ever being in contact with sin. This is never mentioned.
- To then be accepted by God as ransom for the sins of mankind and to be the conqueror of Satan for all eternity.

"Satans altar call "is lies, deceit and death

Christ's altar call is eternal life and joyfulness, and it begins now

Alternative exhibition.
In Norway and in the rest of the world we got something that is simply called alternative help for the human. This is "help" with fortune-telling in cards and healing.
Once every year in Norway there is a alternative exhibition.
There all the alternatives for "helping" the human shows up.
The common theme here is that none of these alternatives got anything to do with Jesus.
God is also used with a capital G. The God we see presented, is under no circumstance The God of the Bible, Who is God Jehovah, Yahweh, which is The Father of Jesus.
Here it is more important than ever in the entire history to be crystal clear on what we believe in. Our faith in Christ must be fine grinded in knowledge, relation, love and Divine intuition, so that we can know the spirits and The Holy Spirit's power. We must be ready at all times.

Get "The stray dog" out.

Chapter 13.

There are many ways to draw near to Satan – Both consciously and unconsciously.

In primitive cultures we find the nature religion. That is to worship just because you have an inner need to do it. Eternity has been put in every human heart. (Ecclesiastes 3, 11). It can be sticks and stones that are worshiped, made a god. When you open up your inner longings in worship of whatever it may be, the demons will come and bind you. This you will not even necessarily notice, before the demons that have you bound, will at some point in time start to bother you and demand things of you. You begin to hear the demons thoughts to you, in your thought life. They will push you with thoughts until you obey. This is a scary thing.

Ouija board, astrology, moving glass and more. There are many things people use to seek contact with the spiritual powers. This is also used as entertainment and party games.

I was not older than 11, when some friends of mine from school and I were home at one of the guys. We wrote down the alphabet with capital letters on a big piece of paper, then we put a glass upside down on it and told the spirits to talk to us. Suddenly the glass started moving from one letter to another. It made words for us to read. Suddenly a window that was shut went open, after closing it, the door burst open. At that point we ended this "game", we did understand that here were things that should not be messed with. What it was, we did not understand as so many others don't. Later on I understood that this were demonic powers manifested to us children. It is terrible, but the reality is there, it is the world of Satan and the demons in the spirit. This works, whether you believe it or not, it is not depending on you.

The daughter of a missionary in China, visited a Buddhist temple as a young girl. She folded her hands and prayed to the Buddha statue, the same prayer that she had heard the monks mumble. Nothing seemed to happen, but from that day she became aware of something alien inside her. There was a scoffing, disdained voice inside of her. Many years later she met a born again Christian which had experience with evil spirits. He laid his hands on her and prayed, and the psychologically pressure that she had experienced for several years was gone.

Get "The stray dog" out

I have prayed for many people in the west and in the third world that have had it in the same way. The demons will enter at first opportunity. Then you need to be set free.

Satan worshipers.
The only important thing that I have not mentioned until now is, Satan worshipers. Satan worshiping is easier to understand. It is simply put, to voluntary make Satan lord of your life.
When you voluntary wishes Satan into your life, you become possessed. This is the only way to become possessed and under complete control of Satan.
If you become possessed, then Satan has full control and you obey every little wink he makes.

Satan worshipers in Stavanger.
This was the place where I first came in contact with worshipers of Satan. A young woman which had been in the satanic environment in that city for some years, came to me. She told me she had been a Satan worshiper and wanted to become free. That again was a completely new experience for me. We agreed to meet up at a parking lot that same night. This was in the autumn

1975, it had become dark, and I arrived at the parking lot.

The ring of fire.
There were not many cars at the parking lot, and it was quiet. Suddenly the young woman showed up and I walked over to her. Without warning a ring of fire appeared around me and her! It had a radius of 4 meters out from where we stood, and was approximately 30cm high all the way around. We were in a way trapped inside this ring of fire!
I realized that Satan wanted to reach me with fear. But I commanded the ring of fire to disappear in The Name of Jesus, and it disappeared immediately! I was glad it worked.

Exorcising demons.
We left the parking lot and went to a place where a friend of mine was waiting, and we were to pray for the woman there. This was the first time I was going to do this. I went straight for it and commanded the spirits to leave her. The woman immediately fell to the floor and started to speak different languages. I recognized some of the different words that she spoke. Satan tried to tire me by saying that he had left her, but still he

Get "The stray dog" out -

remained inside her. We did not give up, but endured. After several hours she was free. This took long time, but it was my first time. We were in a stage of learning that is clear. Here I saw some special, supernatural things manifested.

The ring of fire was a concrete and special manifestation that easily went away in The Name of Jesus. This is manifestations that is not inside the human, but outside. These are easier demons to take down, that is my experience.

If the person performing the exorcism is rooted in the Word, in The Spirit, and lives a life completely surrendered to Christ, then the demons will know the person and Christ in them – and they leave.

The thing is to live a life completely surrendered in a living faith in Christ. It is the simple foundational things in Christ that makes us living disciples of Him. We know what of the supernatural that followed the disciples before the atonement. Now we live after the atonement, and the victory over Satan has been eternally won! The disciples of Jesus became apostles after the atonement. They therefor experienced to live in a victory before, and a total victory after the atonement, and as we also have the full right to live in today.

The woman with a spirit if divination on Likoni island.

The demon python, in the woman with the spirit of divination, knew that the battle was lost, but just wanted to get some attention. The demons in the lead witchdoctor on Zanzibar, got a real surprise. They did not expect to have the power Christ right into the headquarters of the demons on that island. I was on my way down to the ferry from Likoni Island in East-Africa, heading for Mombasa. A woman was standing on a small hill 20 meters away and cried out with all that she had: "Hallelujah, hallelujah, here comes the servant of The God most high". I just kept walking, but it was an experience to remember.

This was the same as Paul experienced with the slave girl with the spirit of divination in Philippi, Macedonia. She cried out: "These men are servants of the Most High God, who proclaim to you the way of salvation."(Acts 16, 16-17)

This slave girl were bothering Paul for several days. Finally he became sick of it,

and commanded the spirit to leave in Christ
Jesus name.
In my case I never saw the woman again
after boarding the ferry, so there were no
reason to do anything with the matter.

Elaboration.
I often experience that demons react to me in
the day to day life, but I can't go on and cast
out demons just because they react. It is just
the way it is supposed to be in a normal
Christian life.

The leading witchdoctor of Zanzibar.
I went to meet this woman, there were set up
an appointment for this meeting. When I
arrived with the video camera hidden in my
bag with the lens sticking out, I was greeted
by 2 bodyguards. I therefor did not get a
chance to film as I had planned, because they
were watching my every move. The
visitation therefor did not go as first planned.
I came into the house of the witchdoctor with
the bodyguards following close.
I thought I had to show a demonstration of
what kind of power that were visiting her
demonized home. I reached out my hand to
greet her, and expected that something
would happen when I did. Immediately her

eyes froze and she took some steps backwards. I walked after, the woman continued to back up against the wall. I continued to take some small steps towards her, and the bodyguards were following. The witchdoctor continued to back up along the wall as long as I kept on walking forward. There was no reason for me to continue the stay, so I said good bye and got past the bodyguards and away. There were at least a demonstration of The Lords Almightiness in the house of the witchdoctor that would create a change. But not for the wellbeing of Satan and the demons.

Foreign languages.
We know that in psychiatry there are several different expressions on different kinds of sufferings. One of them is Schizophrenia. The experience that a person can have several personalities. Each one can reveal themselves with their own behaviour, personality, language and sound. There are also many other psychic ways of expression in psychiatric patients. I have worked for many years in somatic and psychiatry.
On admission- and release meetings with psychiatric patients, we are always a doctor, psychologist and a nurse.

These invisible sicknesses is a mystery within the psychiatry. Medical personnel in psychiatry do their best to soften down the expressions of the psychiatric suffering of the patient, but with small results. The lives of these patients are just a suffering. It is clear to see that God's wisdom and experience, founded upon the written word of God, is the only solution here. It is often shown in meeting with the patients. It gives a clear view and simplicity when you look at it all from God's point of view. At many occasions in the hospital demonic manifestations can be experienced. I can see without a shadow of a doubt, that there are demons causing it. Be it schizophrenia and other psychiatric sufferings. This was also clearly expressed in the woman that was an active Satanist in Stavanger.

Satan worshippers: The dead gets life.
Then the next thing happened. Suddenly several men came in the door and spoke with a monotone voice: "The dead gets life". Then the woman rose up and ran over to them, and they went away. I stood waiting for a short time, but followed after them out and managed to catch up with them further

down the street. Then one of the Satan
worshipers asked me: "Do you have fire?"
I did not answer the question, but laid my
hand on the woman. She fell right on the
ground. Then the Satan worshipers ran
away! I lifted up the woman, and since that
day she has been saved.

Black mass.
In the 17th century a young French lady with
the name of Francoise Montespan, got a
fortune telling lady from Paris to hold a
black mass. The purpose of this was to get
rid of the king's mistress.
The magic that was done, worked. King
Louis the 14th got rid of his younger
mistress, and it is said that the king got rid of
a more beautiful mistress, so that he could be
with Madame de Montespan.
But then Louis got his eyes on a new and
more beautiful lady. And Madame de
Montespan went back to her fortune-telling
friend. A new black mass was held to call
upon the evil spirits, the demons.
And once more Francoise had the king in her
occult grip. But the king had an open eye to
other young beautiful ladies in Paris, so still
a few times more black mass was held in the
black chapel.

Get "The stray dog" out -

Unfortunately for her, a protest was made by the parents of the children that she had sacrificed to keep her position as the king's mistress. When they made a rebellion, an investigation was held, and when king Louis discovered what had happened, he sent Francoise to a nunnery.

Who wanted to be connected to a woman that used magic to seduce?

The fortune-teller and her helper took the blame, before they got executed, they confessed that they had slaughtered over 1500 children in their satanic rituals.

Do not believe for one second that all the women that went for trials during the middle ages were innocent, sweet old ladies. Some of them probably were innocent. You might be saying: This belongs to the past.

The truth is that it is likely more people performing witchcraft today than in the entire history of the world. The interest for witchcraft increased all over the western world in the 1970's. Sacrificing of children are still being performed in secret across the world that we live in.

Get "The stray dog" out -

Chapter 14.

Ways to get bound by Satan and demons – consciously and unconsciously.

1.

1 Reincarnation in the Hinduism, came to the west by gurus, there are 3 big groups:

2 Transcendental meditation, which contains several disguised Hindu techniques to peace and love.

3 The divine light, which is Hindu inspired. "Find god in yourself," is the slogan.

4 The guru Maharishi Mahesh Yogi was the first to come to Norway. His original "spiritual techniques" were changed a bit, to win the western audience, which then became Transcendental Meditation.

2.

1 Buddhism and reincarnation.

2 New Age, a mix of East and West in Hinduism, spiritism and occultism.

3 Mediums, trance mediums and the spiritual existence.

4 Satan worship.

5 Communism.

6 The occult side of Islam.

The Bibles teaching of Jesus Christ reconciliation work and God's plan for salvation in Christ Jesus for us, is simply described in the Bible. The Bible says it itself: "Not even a fool shall go astray." It is that simply put. (I use to say: every genius invention is simple, just look at the cheese slicer and potato peeler). They are simple, but effective and ingenious. And therefore we can also know that the truth, the Bible, is simple and that the lies are complicated, as we see these different alternatives are..

An eternal conglomeration.
Amongst the things mentioned above there is only one thing that most people dissociate from is Satan worship. There are many people that smell and try out the other

Get "The stray dog" out ·

alternatives, and of course some lighter alternatives.

But the one thing they all have in common is that Satan and the demons are behind it. No matter what you believe, this is the truth, the truth of the matter. And more and more Satan and the demons gains influence in the societies of the world, including the Christian congregations. People do not know the difference of things, and therefore most things get accepted.

Witchcraft is tightly bound to astrology and evil spirits.
Spiritism often leads to eastern religions and to reincarnation. And time after time have all this been mixed with drugs, divination and many other things that are forbidden, that has God made very clear through the Bible.

As I see it, Satan and the demons made their last big attack on the west in the late 1960's, and are continuing today.

I am talking about spiritual attacks, and spiritual rape against the citizens of the world's society. The mankind has been tied down spiritually, so that people shall not be able to make an independent spiritual decision, which in turn means the decision to let Christ become LORD in their life.

The faith in Jesus has also been robbed from us, through Satan's use of humanism. We believe more and more in what we are not to believe in, and less and less in what we are to believe in.

Satan and the demons name and number are of no importance.
Listen to what the Bible says: Eph. 6, 12 "For we do not wrestle against flesh and blood, but against the rulers, against the authorities, against the cosmic powers over this present darkness, against the spiritual forces of evil in the heavenly places."

We can further read in Col. 2,15 " He, Jesus, disarmed the rulers and authorities and put them to open shame, by triumphing over them in Him.

Many a Bible school, books and preaching, have told us everything about the different types of demons, ranks and numbers. This I have never understood. I have travelled all over the world and preached the Gospel since I was a young boy.
The demons have always come out under the proclamation of the fantastic victory of Jesus on Calvary. I believe in the victory, and the

Get "The stray dog" out -

demons comes out without any objections.
This has been and is a big part of my life. All
the preaching and teachings about this,
which the Bible does not say so much about,
I consider it less important. Name, number
and rank, has no meaning.
What matters is that the demons are cast out,
and people are set free.
The unbelief in the written Word of God
makes everything so complicated, The Faith
in Gods written Word makes everything
easy.

Get "The stray dog" out -

Chapter 15.

Nature religion you can find in different religions such as occultism and spiritism.

Nature religion.
With nature people we think about people who have a simple form of culture, and live of hunting, livestock or primitive farming. They lack written literature, but they usually have a form of oral tradition with religious content. They are often called primitive people.

Anthropologists.
The anthropologists that have visited them, have written down their impression of the lives and religious practices. By comparing this material from different parts of the world, it has been brought to light relatively similar cultural and religious notion, in cultures with related livelihood and way of living.
When it comes to their notion of God, it can variety, but usually you can find the idea about a higher God. One thinks that He is the last explanation on the mysteries of the existence.

By the side of the highest god, there are always several other gods, and most of all gods that rule over the powers of nature and the life of the animals. As the lord of thunder and rain, fertility deities like "Mother Nature," and gods for hunting, fishing and war.

Among the nature people.
Among the nature people, the worship of **the spirits of the dead plays a huge part. One imagines that the dead lives on in the graves.** From there they go out from time to time, and intervenes with the lives of the living, to means best or sometimes to harm. Sacrifices are made to these spirits to make them have a friendly attitude towards one self. Usually it is the chief who is the highest authority in the cult. By his side there are normally some priests. The priest's task involves not only sacrifice and leading the people in their rituals. They shall interpret signs and cast out spirits.
Especially that last part is important, because one thinks that sickness is caused by possession. **A priest that is particularly involved with exorcising sickness demons, is called a medicine man.**

Among the nature people we always find **the belief in becoming some kind of entity after the death of the body.** The most common thing is the imagination that the human lives on in the underworld as some kind of spiritual being. Sometimes we also meet the belief in soul wandering, that will say the soul returns and into a new born child.

Everything that is, has a god. It's no wonder there is confusion in mankind when it comes to the spiritual. Satan is driving and driving the humankind. Mankind think they have a clear view and control. Which they really don't have at all.

The difference between religion and magic.

The difference between religion and magic is that **in religion the human feels dependent upon the powers that holds their destiny, and they pray to them.** But **in magic they feel like masters over the powers and command them.** The more primitive a society is, the more carefully these two are tied together.

In the nature religion we see the front runner to the western spiritism and we recognize animism.
We can see that the spiritual/demonic has line. A line that sneaks into the western world, were the sense knowing, non-born again human have no prerequisite to understand these realities.

Animism.
Among the people that gets into animism, we find a lot of demon possessed. **Animism is what we call nature religions.** Earlier we found animism only among the more primitive peoples, but it is starting to grow more **and more roots in the modern western culture.**
All men born on the face of the earth, is born with eternity in their hearts. (Ecclesiastes 3,11) – It is because we are created in God's own image and God is Spirit. Our spirit was made unclean due to the fall of man into sin, but it does not hinder that we are created in God's image.
The part that is eternal, our spirit, seeks after the living God Jehovah, Yahweh and His Son Jesus Christ, whether our seeking is conscious or not.

At the same time our unclean spirit seeks after fellowship with its own kind, namely a unclean spirit. On this foundation we have what is called nature religion, animism. Animism (by Latin soul), thus the belief that all objects and phenomenon's in nature have a soul inside it. In further terms the belief in all the thing's impersonal power, <u>mana</u> (animism).

The term animism was originally a part of a philosophical theory.

The term was originally a part of a philosophical theory in Germany in the 17th century, which went like this: The soul was the principle of life and the explanation to the forerunner of the organic universe, in addition to be the carrier of the consciousness.

Within anthropology animism is used about many so called primitive people's religious notions about a soul core in everything.

People that have never heard the Gospel, or even less heard the Name of Jesus, have like everybody else a longing and a need for a spiritual life. A life they were created to live in, even though they are not originally aware of a spiritual life.

That's why every human seek its master.
In nature religion, animism, man worships
and sacrifices to the soul or the powers that
are presumed living in rocks, plants, animals,
dirt, fire, water, thunder, rain and heavenly
bodies with more.
This is done in a longing to have an
unconscious inner spiritual need covered.
The demons sees that the human in their
worship seeks after a spiritual reality. They
then come along with their "satisfaction".
The human gets trapped in the demons grip.
A human that is seeking receives everything
the demons presents to them, and they end
up being strongly bound and controlled. I
write "strongly bound" because there is a
strong affection towards the demons. This is
not a conscious stand to have Satan as lord,
which leads to possession.

Spiritist séance.
In spiritist séances were they use
"mediums", they believe that they through
the medium can contact the spirit of people
that have passed away. This is exactly the
same thing that is being done in nature
religion, animism.
**In these séances it is not a human's spirit
that is summoned, but in fact demons that**

reveals themselves. They pretend to be the person that is tried contacted. They know everything about the person, and can on the basis of that impersonate him/her.

Everything spiritual has its author.
We see clearly that nature religion was the first of all religions. It was the first to come after the fall of man.
The created man's inherent longing after the living God, started to seek. Satan and the demons came to meet it from day one, to catch man's attention.
They did not want man to come in contact with the living God, so they did everything in their power to hinder it.
This you have been explained in the preceding piece.

I want to mention some, about the big religions today.
If we look at Hinduism, which is India's big religion and the Sikh-religion which is an offspring of it, we can quickly see something interesting.
Hinduism have 300 million gods and the Sikhs are in the same group.

Why there are so many gods, is because they see god in everything, (in plants, animals, rocks, yes, in everything.)
Here we recognize animism straight away.

In the normative Islam there is an undercurrent of occultism, if not always visible. This side of Islam is mirrored in the Quran's depiction of powerful, and fast flying spirits. We get to hear about spirit beings that with ease and quickness performs some tasks for king Solomon (Suleiman) that requires some hard work.

They made for him everything he wanted (S34, 12). A powerful spirit (a so called ifrit), is willingly showing up to move the queen of Saba's throne with the speed of lightning (S27, 38f). When it also happens a connection between Solomon's sceptre and these spirits that are eager to serve, we get the impression that the king had a wizard staff or wand with magical powers (S34, 13). On a more common level the magical picture of Solomon is explained by the amulet "The seal of Solomon".
The common Islam are stressing that this action protects against the powers of evil spirits. It is impossible for normative Islam

Get "The stray dog" out

to get rid of people's occult understanding in this matter, because this understanding is legitimized by Muslim oral tradition (Hadith).

It is told that the great Sufi theologian al-Ghazali, once got help from a conjurer. About that experience he says: "I saw the spirits as shadows on a brick wall." He did not make a stand against the occult, but sought contact with this reality.

If we go to spiritism and occultism, we see the belief and the practice of the belief in the contact with the spirits of the dead. One also imagines that the deceased live on in the graves. Here we recognize something from voodoo.

One can clearly see that every religion, spiritism and occultism got its origin in nature religion.

Explaining appendix.
Theosophy. (Of Theo and Greek wisdom) Religious belief that builds on nature mysticism and that God exists in all things. In 1875, Helene Petronova Blavatsky (1831-91) founded a society in USA by the name of Theosophical Society. The goal was to spread a teaching she had written down, a

mix of Indian, Egyptian and European
traditions.

Prominent in this teaching, is gradually
development of mankind through
reincarnation (as Hinduism), and the belief
in a universal intelligence which is being
managed by the so called <u>mahatmas</u>,
unworldly masters which teaches the
humans.

Helena Petronova Blavatsky became also an
important piece for the New Age movement
with her teachings.

Annie Besant (1847-1933) became leader of
the society after Helena Blavatsky's death.
She was also one of the leaders in the Indian
congress party (Indian National Congress).
The Theosophists got great influence in
India. They were often negative towards
Christianity.

**Were Marx, Stalin, Hitler and Mao
involved in the occult?**

Everybody knows that **Karl Marx** is the
original father of communism and marxist
socialism. And no one of the so called
"intellectuals" in the last generations have
made so deep blood covered footprints in
mankind as he did.

He is also the author of "The communist manifesto" which became like the bible to communism and socialism. This he wrote in London. Not many people know that Karl Marx also was a poet. By studying Marx as a poet, we get to know an unpleasant keynote in Marx life and teachings – and can make out the contour of the evil mastermind. Paul Johnson writes in his book "intellectuals", that the main themes in Marx poems were destruction, hate, an attraction to corruption and violence, suicide pacts, and pacts with the devil.

This sounds identical to our times Satan worship and occultism.

People that study Marx have lately been taken more up by his poetry. They study his personality and the origin of his revolution. Out of these studies there are now coming shocking claims that Karl Marx worshiped Satan.

In Marx contemporary there were a flourishing of Satan worship.

Intellectuals, writers, artists, philosophers, and revolutionaries were often attending spiritist séances, occult rituals and satanic masses in salons and aristocratic parties, in the cultural capitols of Europe.

In the book "Marx and Satan", Richard Wurmbrand underpins strong evidence of how Marx hated God and preferred Satan in God's place. Wurmbrand is presenting convincing circumstantial evidence that Marx worshiped Satan. Also in the communistic Soviet have occultism and Satan worship flourished all the way to the top in party circles.

This is often shown on TV in Soviet in the time before and just after glasnost.
It was a heritage after the first communists. **As with Marx the occult also played an important part in the lives of Stalin, Hitler and Mao.** Mao in spite his public atheism, which the other world destroyers also had, they were very superstitious. (Fallen gods, 1998)

Another comparison to mention is the one between Adolf Hitler and the medium John of God. They were both as young boys visited by demons. Hitler was visited by "the virgin Mary" a demon portraying an "angel of light", who **made** him believe he was to become "the saviour of the world". Already back then it is likely that Hitler got bound in his personality by demons.

A young fortune-telling lady in the mountains of Human, prophesied that Mao were to become a great leader, prime minister or chief of bandits. "You can kill hundred thousand without blinking an eye," the lady prophesied. The same thing did most likely happen to Mao here.

When it comes to getting into service for the kingdom of God, we see that people are often chosen from a young age. The same thing we can see Satan do, he is a "copycat" all the way. **John of God** got into his demonic service already at the age of 9. Then he got a **premonition,** or as spiritual gifts will call it, a word of knowledge or word of wisdom.

Satan and the demons will always try to copy everything God does. Satan and the demons cannot under any circumstance create anything original. They can to a certain amount copy what God does, but of course without the power of The Holy Spirit. It has to do with Satanic/demonic power.

John of God grew up in a catholic and spiritis home. A lot of Catholics have this combination in their faith.

As I see it, he must not have thought that it was Satan and the demons that revealed themselves for him through saints. He must have believed they were helpers, energies that he would be the channel/medium for. He grew up in a spiritual mess and did not think further than this.

From the Bible we can clearly see that this is the work of Satan and the demons.

Sometime later, John of God felt depressed and was weakened by hunger. He lived in poverty. He then took shelter under a bridge in the outskirts of his town,and walked down to the river under the bridge, Then a beautiful lady called out for him. She told him to come closer.

They spent one afternoon together in conversation. The next morning he remembered the young lady's beauty and mildness, and got drawn down to the river again for another conversation. He got amazed when he noticed a shining strip of light were she had sat down. He got even more astonished, when she called him by name.

See the likeness of how Satan chose Adolf Hitler and John of God.

Get "The stray dog" out

Chapter 16.

The occult – Islam's hidden side.
When novelist Margit Sandemo describes
and glorifies a reality of spirits and magical
powers, we can draw parallels the
understanding of reality we meet in African
animism and the common Islam.
In the normative Islam there is an
undercurrent of occultism, if not always
visible. This side of Islam is mirrored in the
Quran's depiction of powerful, and fast
flying spirits. We get to hear about spirit
beings that with ease and quickness performs
some tasks for king Solomon (Suleiman) that
requires some hard work.
They made for him everything he wanted
(S34, 12). A powerful spirit (a so called
efreet), is willingly showing up to move the
queen of Saba's throne with the speed of
lightning (S27, 38f). When it also happens a
connection between Solomon's scepter and
these spirits that are eager to serve, we get
the impression that the king had a wizard
staff or wand with magical powers (S34, 13).
On a more common level the magical picture
of Solomon is explained by the amulet "The
seal of Solomon".

The common Islam are stressing that this action protects against the powers of evil spirits. It is impossible for normative Islam to get rid of people's occult understanding in this matter, because this understanding is legitimized by Muslim oral tradition (Hadith).

It is told that the great sufi theologian al-Ghazali, once got help from a conjurer. About that experience he says: "I saw the spirits as shadows on a brick wall." He did not make a stand against the occult, but sought contact with this reality.

Muhammad.

One thing is Muhammad's radical dealing with polytheism. The other thing is his lack of dealing with the occult. Sources indicates that Muhammad used magical incantations to protect himself from evil. The two last surahs in Quran (S113 and 114) are good examples of this. The surahs are called "cries for shelter and protection".

The book "The jinn in the Quran and the Sunna" (Ashour 1989), gives us a vivid picture of Muhammad's relation to the spirit world. The book confirms that Islam has a fully developed teaching on spirits- and demons, which is adhered in this time.

Get "The stray dog" out

The common understanding of the jinn's, is that they are real and active spiritual beings. It is said that they are placed in the earth's sphere, the skies. Amongst common Muslims the spiritual world is a big universe of anxiety. Among the Arabs it is normal to call the spirits for "Those people" (hazdu al-nas), but among the Iranians calls them "those that are better than us" (az ma biharan). In the Muslim consciousness the spirits are close to the humans and can be influenced, whilst Allah is distant and hardly lets himself be influenced. From the outside it can look contradictory to combine the worship of spirits and the Muslim faith and practice.

Some years ago, in one of the villages on the islands of the Comoros, A public meeting was held in the mosque. They were to discuss the case of spirit sermons. After some discussion it was settled that they were not to hold any spirit sermons on the night to Friday. There is a need for us to think through our standing with spiritual phenomenon's in general, the problem of possession especially.

Islam's belief in spirits is totally opposite the western view on reality. The "secular" understanding of reality gives little space for

invisible spirits. Also within the Norwegian
Church in newer times, one has been
characterized with this "view of reality
without spirits". But the rise of many new
religious societies in our own backyard, has
given a total change to the spiritual climate.
We must get a balanced understanding, were
we take the battle against the devil and his
spirit army seriously, but at the same time
avoid hysteria and speculations.

The Bible takes into account spiritual beings
and spiritual powers, the spirits are beings
with personality, which can speak and
believe. (Mark. 5, 9 James 2,19).

When a Muslim conjurers tell that they can
get spirits to find missing items or reveal
thieves, then there are no reasons to doubt
the possibilities for this. (jf. 1 Sam 28,8ff)
When Islam talks about "good spirits" and
Margit Sandemo talks about "helpers", then
we are dealing with satanic seduction. (jf. 2.
Kor 11, 14) in reality it is the spiritual forces
of evil in the heavenly places they are talking
about. (Eph. 6, 12)

So in the meeting with Muslims it is
important that we come with liberating
power of the Gospel. It exists suffering that
is far beyond the bounds of medical
knowledge. These are sufferings that can

only be cured by spiritual means. **Muslim theologians have problems seeing the line between forbidden and permitted magic.**

Get "The stray dog" out ·

Chapter 17.

"You shall have no other gods before me, and you shall not make yourself any carved image or any likeness
of that which is up in heaven or of that which is down on earth, or that which is down in the water below the earth. You shall not worship them nor serve them."(Exodus 20, 3-4).
These 2 commandments are not to make you a bond servant, but to make sure that the demons can't bind you.
Who is going to watch over us, if we don't allow God Yahweh to watch over us, through Christ Jesus and His written Word, The Bible? Now I'm going to mention something about a few of Satan's ambushes. Just remember that everything I write about is not to scare you, but to give you understanding, which makes you capable of exposing Satan and the demons. When you have exposed them you got authority over them in Jesus name. If that isn't great, then I don't know.

Animism.
The word animism comes from the Latin word anima, which means soul or breath.

A higher power and the supernatural world. What lies as a base to animism is that the supernatural is stronger than the human. They believe that a higher power lives inside certain objects, as trees, rocks, flowers, animals or places like in a forest, or in a village. Sometimes the spirits makes an action. They even move around when people do it.

The origin of spirits.
They believe that some spirits are the souls of deceased forefathers. Other are creations linked to nature and the supernatural world. For some, the spirit is the intermediaries between man and higher gods.
This is often the case in the common religions, or the primary religions who acknowledges one god that is above everyone else. In other primary religions the spirits are mainly beings in the supernatural reality. Help like this is often sought after. Sometimes the help from some particular spirits are sought after for some particular occasions, like, when sick, war, marriage, child birth or for work or studying. They also seek help when they need help to change the weather or for a good harvest. (You

understand that this is the spiritist and occult side, not the truth. The truth is the Bible!)

The relation with the spirits.
The relation between the supernatural world and the human world is constant, and requires human effort. Some spirits are looked upon as friendly minded and helpful, and gratitude is shown by prayer or sacrifice. Other spirits can be evil or make troubles, these are to be avoided or pleased. Human effort is needed to make sure they have goodwill with the spirits, and to make sure they are no longer offended or ignored.

Contact with the spirits.
To contact the spirits certain methods or trained persons are needed, gifted individuals are often required. Some tribes have a shaman. The shaman gets in contact with the spirit world through a trance. They return to the physical world with a message from the spirits. Other societies gets contact through a medium or divination. Divination methods include astrology (as an example, China), fortune telling (as an example, by a selection of written fortune in the common Buddhism) and rituals (in many tribe societies). In many areas, also were the world religions are

established, there are local healers that use rituals so that sick people can get healed by spirits. In villages they will also use nature methods (plants and bushes), which they believe have spiritual powers.

The animism's invisible bondage of people in the western world.

The invisible bindings of animism we can see all over the Western world. The Western world is more materialistic oriented than spiritually oriented. This makes people in the west easy preys to the demons in different degrees. The focus of materialism, which makes the material things into some type of false idol, gives the demons a great opportunity to enter with their addiction. Here there are of course just as many varieties as there are people, but the demons are the same. The bindings of the demons will add more problems to the person that is bound.

In the third world we see obvious sufferings of people that worships sticks and stones, either it is when seeking help or when they try to please the demons they fear.

In the West this is entirely different. Here people worship everything from the big new home-media-centre, with TV, PC, music system and so on. Or the new cars and not to forget the renovation/redecoration of the already nice house, from time to time. This sounds completely human like and normal, isn't that nice? There are no demons in this? Dear friend, everything is spiritual, what you adulate (that was a white washed word for worship, right?) has power over you!

It is not the car, the house or the music system, but the demon behind it, which makes you addicted to this. You are dominated and controlled, it is not a pleasant thing.

Fetishism.

What is it? The psychology of fetishism is as follows: Every object can be a god - if you just tell the object that it is god. Fetish means artificial.

It is an object that is added supernatural powers, or an object created by humans, which is added power over others.

A simple example from Africa. A man is going to buy something of a substantial amount. He looks for a god that can help him, and suddenly something completely natural lies in front of him. It can be anything, like a rock. He then promises to give up an offering of flowers each day to the rock, the deal goes sweet, and the African man has got a new god to worship. A god that probably can help him with other stuff also. And now comes the danger. Now he asks the stone for help in his next deal also. The thing that now happens is that he opens up his inner being to a spiritual dimension, a spiritual world. It is not God Jehovah who comes, but demons, and the bindings have started to happen in the personality of the African man. Do you see how easy it happens?

The beginning of nature religion.
In earlier (western) depictions of nature religions, they have often been characterized as "primitive". Among other things due to to the fact that most of them comes from cultures without a written language.
The term nature religion suggests that they first and foremost worshiped nature in different kind of ways. E.g. the sun, animals or trees. This is accurate for some, but far from all nature religions. There are also common with worship of gods, spirits, and ancestors so on. You can therefor divide nature religion into groups, e.g. animism, shamanism, monotheism, polytheism, veneration of ancestors and more. Before the

spreading of today's world religions, it is most likely that the nature religions existed in every culture or society. Today they are still common in certain regions in Africa, America and round the polar circle, including Finnish, Ugric religions in Sapmi and Siberia. It is estimated that a quarter to half a billion people believe in nature religions.

1000 years from the fall of man to the start of Hinduism.

Joshua 24,2 "And Joshua said to all the people, "Thus says the Lord, the God of Israel, 'Long ago, your fathers lived beyond the Euphrates, Terah, the father of Abraham and of Nahor; and they served other gods.

Here we see in the book of Joshua, what we also can see in the books that Moses wrote. The idol worship was something that came into the world very soon after the fall of man. It flourished and spread for several hundred years, until year 1000 when Hinduism took form.

Hinduism have approximately 20 main gods, and under them 300 million lesser gods. Their worship of false idols was all nature religion. They saw soul and life in everything. Everything that brought them something positive, they made into a god for worship and offerings. If you now, like it has been done for thousands of years, worship sticks and stones, then you give an opening for the demons to enter in, take control and bind these people.

In nature religion in Africa we can find calling on the dead. It is not the dead that are being conjured, but demons. This is spiritism, yes occultism. The nature religion in Africa is the same as in Hinduism, sticks and stones are worshiped and the demons answers the call. They that go deeper into Africa, goes over to Satan worship, witchcraft and sorcery.

We see clearly that before Christ came, worshiping of false idols had been in the world for almost 4000 years.

Think about how Satan has made use of his opportunities since the fall of man. He has worked determined to catch all of mankind, since approximately the fall of man. The victory of Jesus Christ on Calvary has been available for 2000 years.

It's an interacting of the satanic/demonic world and those that follow the rulers and authorities, the spiritual forces of evil in the heavenly places. They have worked actively with mankind since day 1.

But the good news are here, and has been here for 2000 years. Jesus Christ has won the victory for us all! Let us get these good news out with the power of The Holy Spirit, to the remaining unreached world, so that Christ can return!

The burning of fetishes on crusades around the world.

Burning fetishes is something that I have always done on crusades around the world. The fetishes are collected on several of the meetings held during a crusade. People have taken the fetishes off when they have given their lives to Jesus, so that they get burned. It happens often that people gets choked by the amulets they wear around their neck, when they want to give their lives to Jesus. My fellow workers must often cut off the collars or necklaces with the fetishes. Joyful shouts reaches the skies when people experience that the fear, the compulsion and the curse has been broken, and the fetishes are being burnt. I collect all the fetishes and add a little gasoline, so that we can get a powerful manifestation of the victory over the demons and liberation of the people that were bound. People have thought that the fetish has been their servant, but the demon in the fetish has demanded service back. The carrier of the fetish has become slave to the demon. The fetishes are hidden on the body, if they are not worn around the neck. My meetings have always been filmed, also the burning of the fetishes. TV- stations have shown tapes of fetish burning in their news reports in prime time on African television. It has been both before and after prayers in mosques. This has drawn great attention from both the spiritual world and the physical world.

The demons reveal themselves quickly and they come out with loud screams. While I am preaching during campaigns, those that are being tormented by demons always start to scream. My fellow workers breaks their way through the crowds and brings them out. I have always a place prepared behind the platform were they are laid down, and they get help removing the fetishes. The demons comes out with loud screams, shivers and vomiting. The fetish is a hangout for a powerful spirit, which the carrier can call upon when he is in need, or wishes to do something supernatural. One has to treat the spirits carefully, because they have power over both life and death, for those that believe and carries the fetishes. On my last crusade to Africa, with 100 000 people gathered, I just couldn't speak, but stood at the edge of the platform with both hands raised towards the skies.

Then the people that were bound and being tormented started running towards the platform. They were many, they ripped off their fetishes and fell on the ground, screaming, shaking, vomiting and rolling around. After a while everything got quiet, the demons had left them. Now it was time to pray for salvation!

It is difficult for most people to take witchcraft seriously.

It probably is hard to do that, we that live in such a materialistic, superficial world. Many children today associate Halloween-night with black cats, brooms and pumpkins. Many people think that the witches are nice. Over 300 years ago, under the inquisition, witches and others got burnt alive. This was terrible. But it is not any worse on our light attitude we have today towards the spiritual world and harmless poking in the occult.

I mentioned a story about black mass earlier in the book, I want to mention one more black mass, also from the 14th century.
It was John V, the duke of Bretagne, who got dozens of complaints from parents that accused the Baron of Retz of stealing their children. The duke investigated the complaints and discovered that the baron and his friends collected children to sacrifice under black mass.
As most things that has to do with witchcraft, black mass is hidden deep in the dark, so it is hard to tell were the truth ends and the illusion begins. But still there are some clear facts about how one was most likely being performed, in Europe during the Middle Ages.
In a black draped chapel stood black candles on a black altar which was covered in black. Upon the altar laid a naked woman with a cross between her breasts, and a chalice between her thighs.
With a hostile stolen from a Christian church, an undressed priest held the mass. The main event in the mass was the sacrifice of an animal or a child.

Witchcraft got so many forms today, that it is hard to keep up with it all. I have heard of

a group of witches that surpasses the
women's liberation movement.
Their only goal in life is to vanquish men –
by getting revenge on them. When these
witches meet, they conjure evil spirits to hurt
or destroy different men.

Get "The stray dog" out -

Chapter 18.

Witchdoctors and warlocks.

They gave themselves completely to Satan.
They gave themselves completely to Satan
and laid everything in his hands. The heart
wanted only one thing: to be filled with him.
In their despair they crave for a saviour, but
gets completely fooled and manipulated by
Satan.
In the middle of the night in the thickest
darkness, Satan comes to his servants. One
could hear him filling up each one. Then the
passionate and obtrusive prayer gets replaced
by some horrific screams.
There was no doubt of who it was that came.
This is witchdoctors and witches own story
about their reality in Ethiopia.
From the top of their lounges they scream:
"He has arrived, he has arrived."
What a tragedy, but true.

Many conceives warlocks as frauds.
Many conceives witchdoctors or warlocks as
frauds, who with a lot of means torments and
afflicts people, to pretend to heal them. But
here you will soon realize that it is not the
entire truth. "I have healed many," says the

witchdoctor, "but I could not have done it without Satan".

Satanic and demonic examinations
Witch doctors and warlocks work together. When they worship or perform "agga". This is what they call it, when they run into a fire and out again without getting burn marks. The warlock and witchdoctor test is a red hot knife pressed on each chin and on the back of the hand. If no blisters or burn become visible, then the person is accepted as witchdoctor and warlock.

Cut the head off a snake and whip people with the body of the snake.
The worst thing that can happen with a person when a witchdoctor comes to visit, is if he cuts the head off a snake and start to whip the person with the body of the snake. Satan gets angry every time someone kills a snake. He makes a terrible revenge and brings a curse on the person that has been whipped with the snake. It means death and curse upon the person's family.
Much of the things done by witchdoctors and warlocks can be revealed as humbug, but not absolutely everything. Satan is for real, and so are the demons.

Get "The stray dog" out

Chapter 19

The biggest spiritual crisis in 2000 years is here now.

My experience of the age we are living in right now, is that we now are in mankind's biggest spiritual crisis. Wilburn M. Smith said in the book "World crisis and the prophetic Scripture" (Chicago, Moody press, 1951): "Mankind is preparing to submit to demonic influence in a way that has never occurred in modern times."

When I in the 80's was together with Lester Sumrall in his church in Southbend, Indiana in U.S.A, and spoke there, we talked about these things. We did also make a TV-program about this that aired all over North-America, Honolulu and Hawaii.

"Listen here, Tom." said Lester Sumrall to me, "Christians are going to see angels that are with them and helping them. It will also be more demonic activity than ever before. It will be more repressed and possessed people than ever before."

The less it is talked about and known about Satan and the demons, the more pleased Satan is. It makes us incapable to see the works of Satan and the demons in our daily lives. Satan can then easily intertwine tightly

with our state of existing, as he has now
done.

If we read in Gal. 5,17-21, we see that the
works of the flesh are mentioned. I will add
it for you:
"For the desires of the flesh are against the
Spirit, and the desires of the Spirit are
against the flesh, for these are opposed to
each other, to keep you from doing the
things you want to do. But if you are led by
the Spirit, you are not under the law. Now
the works of the flesh are evident: sexual
immorality, impurity, sensuality, idolatry,
sorcery, enmity, strife, jealousy, fits of
anger, rivalries, dissensions, divisions, envy,
drunkenness, orgies, and things like these. I
warn you, as I warned you before, that those
who do such things will not inherit the
kingdom of God."

Yes, here you got a list of things that we all
recognize from our day to day life. Mankind
doesn't view this as demonic manipulation
and control. Exactly to get people to do these
negative things, to break down humanity.
"These things are a part of the human," we
say. There are good people and there are bad
people. Yes, that is true, but how have they

Get "The stray dog" out

become evil? Yes, exactly through the things I have described for you from the Bible. These simple Bible verses and their containing of the truth, has and is Satan using to break down mankind. Sit down and ponder on every one of the works of the flesh which are mentioned here in the Bible, then you will recognize them all. You will see that it is exactly these that breaks down the world today. Originally man has no desire to be like this, but they become like this.

Mankind under attack.
Mankind is under constant attack from the spiritual world. Satan's wild card is that the human doesn't believe he exists! Everything is just "human", good and bad people. Talk about being deceived! The lie is being believed instead of the truth, the woven blanket with Satan in every other thread, becomes tighter and tighter!
The planet Tellus, the earth, which were supposed to be the Garden of Eden, a paradise, has Satan gained access to and made into his own personal torture chamber.

The Bible says in John. 10,10-:"Satan comes to steal, murder and destroy."

It does not have to be this way. Instead of being channels and mediums for Satan, we can become channels and mediums for God, Jehovah, through His Son Jesus Christ. Because of the works of victory He did over Satan, once and for all, on Calvary.

The Western world has viewed the third world countries as primitive in all its existence and their understanding of reality. They have spirituality and primitive religions as centre in their environment. They have not had the same possibility as we do when it comes to the material way.
Therefor they have sought out the other way and found realities there, which we in the West have denied. But now everything has come upon us in the West also. When the West finally gets their eyes open to it, they will find themselves bound by Satan and the demons.

The church under attack.
What has become the biggest tragedy in all of this, is that Christian congregations, churches, has a strong infiltration of Satan and demonic powers. It doesn't help one bit to call yourself a Christian, if you are not

Get "The stray dog" out -

born again and have Jesus as the real Lord of your life.

Then we will, as many other non-Christians, become victims of the evil in many different ways.

Not every supernatural thing that happens is the Lords doing.

The level of spiritual insight among the Christians world over, is of such low level that the Christians are no match for the demons. I hear about it everywhere, and experience it myself, how the demons find their ways into the Christian congregations. Once inside they put their plans into action and does whatever it takes to break down the Christian fellowship. The Christians are so carnal, that they have no idea what's going on. (Gal 5,16-21). And they are not even close in having the ability to discern spirits (1.Cor. 12,10), Which is an absolute necessity, now more than ever in the entire history of man.

Not every supernatural thing that happens among Christians is a work of The Lord, but they believe that. It can't become more depressive than this. A giant of the spirit has to stand up among the Christians world over, in Christ Jesus! That is our hope. If these

spiritual qualities shall benefit us, we have to
undress the works of the flesh and dress up
in the fruits of The Holy Spirit. (Gal 5,22).
It's these simple but yet so difficult things
that has to be done in the lives of the
Christians, if we want to walk hand in hand
with victory at all times. The Christians have
to clean their own home before anything can
be done outwards with success and victory.

How Satan and the demons gets to use us.
The works of the flesh we read in the letter
to the Galatians, is a result of that we as
humans, through our senses receives the
thoughts and feelings of Satan and the
demons and live them out.
Our psyche, soul, spirit and body are under
constant attack. An example that is easy to
understand: A man is standing trial for the
murder of another human being. He can tell
the judge that he just couldn't stop himself
from killing, it was such a great necessity,
like an urge that pushed him to it. He would
not had peace before he had done it.
Isn't it about time that we open up our inner
eyes and confess that there is a spiritual
world that we have to relate to. In the way
that I just explained, is it that Satan and the
demons use us. The world of the spirit uses

Get "The stray dog" out -

our thought life and our feelings, yes all our senses.

The good news are here – We ourselves decide what we let into us, or what we allow ourselves to do, or not to do. This is the simple explanation of why we are where we are in this day's society.

The occult harvest – Satan and the demons got their scythes out for harvest.
We no longer sit alone in the West with our Christianity, with big blue eyes and sing Christmas carols. No, that time has passed. The war has intensified in the spiritual world. All the world's religions and occult ways has come to our doorstep. We have to take stands that we did not have to before. We don't enjoy doing it, but we have to for our own sake.

Satan and the demons got their scythes out for harvest. In this book I have mentioned things from strong occult movements, to show the gravity of Satan's and the demons tight braiding into our world. It is a strong "altar call" from Satan. Let us take charge, the victory is ours in the Name of Jesus.

Chapter 20.

Spirituality or the flesh.

In my 40 years as a Christian I think the Christian life world over, in the degree I have seen it, has spiralled down. "That was a negative statement," you might be saying, or perhaps you say that I am right. I for one believe that this is the situation.

It has popped up several bible schools, modern churches, nice choirs and many more "trendy" preachers than I have ever seen before. It doesn't matter with correct doctrine and that we say that we are under "the anointing", whatever that is, if we are not in The Holy Spirit, I mean in the spiritual world.

We have 2 worlds we can move in. We got the physical world and the spiritual world. My personal experience, without coming on to strong, is that the Christians move in the physical world, in the flesh, while the occult moves in the spiritual world. Have you ever thought about that?

"In the spirit and under the anointing"

When preachers claim to be "in the spirit and under the anointing" from the podium, while people in the room only experience them being in the flesh – what happens then? Yes, that is an interesting question. Here at least there is a group of people that understands the difference between spirit and flesh.

But what about those that don't understand what they experience, it goes both ways, it doesn't seem real, there is something strange, they get confused, insecure? They don't know what to believe anymore.

A position like this, which there are plenty of, should never have been. The occult are spiritual, but in the wrong spirit, while the Christians that have the right Spirit, are not in the Spirit!

It just can't be like this.

Every Christian has of course responsibility for his own Christian growth and understanding. We have all we need in the Bible, but the Bible tells us crystal clear in the book of 1. Corinthians about the different gifts of service.

Pastor and teacher.

Among these we have a service which is called pastor and one that is called teacher. These gifts have a special function to take care of those part of the body of Christ, which is not in an evangelistic service. A combination of responsibility for themselves

as Christians, and a pastor/teacher
responsibility for the body of Christ, I think
can be a nice combination and a necessity.
To preach from the podium, and to proclaim
one is in the Spirit, while the truth is that
everything is in the flesh, is a dangerous
combination. Think of what a danger this is
to people that hungers for the Lord Jesus and
revelation of His glory. Here it will be a
great opportunity for demons to come and
defile the presence of the body of Christ, and
potentially those that want to be a part of that
body.

Get in the position of the spirit.
As Christians we have to get into a spiritual
position with our lives. This is something we
just HAVE TO. If not we will not only
destroy for ourselves but for those around us.
We all have a contagious effect both in the
physical and in the spiritual, and we don't
have to bring bad spiritual quality. The
Christian is his own worst enemy. Truth be
told, Satan and the demons are no hard
match, so what are we doing about that?

What is the answer?
The answer is a spiritual awakening! By that
I mean that those that are born again have to

Get "The stray dog" out -

seek with all their heart and become spiritual. Satan and the followers of the evil demons are spiritually aware. It is those that are born again that should be the absolute spirituals! Those that stand in the power of The Holy Spirit and defeats every demon at any time in the world of the Spirit!

Those that are born again – should be the absolute spiritual!

Get "The stray dog" out ·

Chapter 21.

Is everything impossible? - Yes, if we don't repent and believe.

Admit to yourself that there is a spiritual world which is in control. Have you done that, so choose to be on the right side? You have a choice here, the only thing that might hinder you to choose Christ, is your pride. If you are proud, it is not easy to choose Christ, because you are the one that fixes everything and is not afraid to die when that day comes.

Yes, it is good that you are clever and have control of your life and don't fear what comes after death.

You might believe that there is nothing after death. All this is fine. But anyhow, there is a spiritual world, and we live for all eternity anyways.

No matter what you believe or do, it is the Spirit's world that controls everything eternally. You think on that one.

Will Jesus return?

It is a question well worth asking in these days. If we look around us, it doesn't look so bright. People have for several years prophesied and preached about Jesus second coming in their lifetime. Many of them have passed away and Jesus has still not come. Many lives and believes He is just around the corner.

I don't believe that, I believe that Jesus second coming dials itself in according to how the church of Christ here on earth behaves, and carries out the task we have been given by Jesus (Mark. 16,15).

Christianity all over the world bows for Satan, and one strange doctrine after the other pops up.

It is only one guarantee for Jesus soon coming – who can stop the occult onslaught?
It is by obeying the command of Christ and acting with the power and boldness of The Holy Spirit. Proclaiming the victory of the gospel with earth shaking and spirit shaking power, so that the gospel which is a power of God (Rom 1, 16) can reach every nation, so that Christ can return.
We need a spiritual earthquake. Satan is defeated, but we have to throw him out together with all the demons, so that the

Get "The stray dog" out

proclamation of the gospel can reach all human beings and Christ can return.

We can and have to stop the occult onslaught.
Read Mark 16, 15-18. Matthew 24, 14 and Matthew 28, 18-20.

A new dark age.
It is not to smile at, shrug at or dismiss. It can be closer than you thing. The beginning of a long – long new dark age. Different than the first, but a dark age of Divine darkness and of that which follows in the footsteps of darkness.

A new interrogation (inquisition) can come, but it is all up to us, we that claim to be born again and filled by The Holy Spirit's power.

The occult onslaught can be avoided if we see our responsibility.

The victory can come sooner than you think.
By and large the Christian world has not understand the gravity in the victory of Christ and what dimension the victory has been set in. What we do in our meetings, is for the most things that Satan is ok with.

What happens is of no threat to him. For they
know not their enemy.

The alternative groups world over, have
understanding and knowledge of the spiritual
world. Many of them move in the spiritual
world, but they move on the side of Satan
and are completely manipulated and living a
lie. They are in the spirit, which I cannot say
about what I see the Christians are, which
absolutely should be there on God Jehovah's
(Yahweh's) side, and carry forth the victory
of Christ and live in it all day, all year.

We must get into position.
It is not a manic stress, but it's a life you
work your way in position to.
It has to become a natural part of our
presence in life. The Christians, as far as I've
seen, live their lives only on the "surface" of
the spiritual life.
That is also the cause to why the world is
like it is today. If we would have lived in the
Spirit, we would by the victory in the Spirit,
changed the world into the position God
wants it to be. Namely: The gospel out to
everyone so that Jesus Christ can return!
We have to have a victorious life in the
Spirit.

Mark. 16, 15 Jesus said: "Go into all the world and proclaim the gospel to the whole creation."

Get "The stray dog" out -

Chapter 22.

God's breakthrough power in Jesus Christ. (Your foundation for victory.)

Mark. 16, 15
Jesus commanded His disciples: "Go into all the world and proclaim the gospel to the whole creation."

What is the most important message in the world?
There are many voices, today as before, who claims to have an important message to the world. But it is only one message that is the most important one, and which is the truth (John. 14, 6): it is the **gospel**. And it was exactly this message Jesus told His disciples (which is me and you that are living whole heartedly for Him) to go into **all** the world and proclaim.
One can preach on great and long theological correct messages, from Genesis to the book of revelation without preaching the gospel. It is no problem for someone who got a little theological insight.
Think about it: 200 years after Jesus had returned to His Father in heaven, the whole world of that time had been evangelized.

They had no TV or radios to spread the gospel with, neither did they have cars or airplanes to move quickly from place to place.

How did they manage to do that?
We have not managed to get the message out to the world of our time, even though we have all these technological gadgets to help us. **They just simply proclaimed the gospel,** they did not proclaim a religion or new lifestyle.
They gave the gospel to the people. And that is the secret. **If all proclamation being preached had been the gospel, then the world of our time would have been evangelized. But it is not.**

God doesn't "stand up" for preaching about what we THINK about Him. He doesn't "stand up" for any human "I understand this" explaining theology.
God will only "stand up" for ONE thing – and that is the GOSPEL. But not any kind of gospel." The Gospel" means good news.
Many people say they have good news, but it is only one message that is the true, good news.

And that is: The good news about Jesus
Christ, God Yahweh's living Son.

Listen to what the Bible says in Rom. 1,16.
"The gospel, **is** the power of God for
salvation to everyone who believes"

I want to comment this verse for you.
The gospel, as I have already told, **means**
good news.
We divide up the verse.
Is means: not **was**, or **is going to be**, but it
means **is now**.
The power of God means: **The complete
work of Jesus on Calvary.**
For salvation means: **The complete
liberation of spirit, soul and body.**
To everyone who believes means: **Receives
the message and acts on the victory that is
already won. Agrees to it and does it, and
will then experience the result of that
victory which one partakes in.**

The Bible says in 1.Corinth 1,18
"For the word of the cross is folly to those
who are perishing, but to us who are being
saved it **is** the **power of God.**"

Meeting with the students in college.
I especially remember a meeting at a school in Norway. About 350 students were attending. Only a few of those were born again, thus Christians. Satan was scared to death of that meeting. He was afraid the students would hear the truth about the gospel.
On the front row seats people that denied Christ had gathered. They had decided to "break" the one that were to preach.
These youths were tools in the hand of Satan, whether they knew it or not.
It is a spiritual reality we live in, which controls everything. It sounds bad and it is bad.
I gave the crowd the truth about Jesus Christ, Gods living Son, I gave them Gods power. And it did not lack result. God "stands up" for the gospel of His Own Son, and nothing else. The whole room came in motion.
Things were thrown at me from the crowd, and "the Christ deniers" at the front row cowherds their ears and yelled just like in the Bible. It was a demonstration of Gods power at that school, and the effect lasted for a long time afterwards.

Get "The stray dog" out

As long as there is just human opinions of the Word of God that is preached, The Holy Spirit will not be active with His power, and reactions like this will never be experienced. But in the moment we are going for the proclamation of God's Word, preach Christ, and we stand firm in the faith in with we preach, the reactions will come.

Yes, the demonstration of Gods power and a breakthrough in the world of the Spirit, which again gives results here in the natural, sensible world.

It has never been power in the cross, but only in the man that hung there. (Gal 3,13).

The Bible says in John. 3, 16.
"For God so loved the world, that he gave his only Son, that whoever believes in him should not perish but have eternal life."

We have the message to a world in disorder – The message about the Man on the cross, Jesus Christ, Gods living Son.

Many people walked past the eminence at Calvary, they saw Jesus Christ hanging there.

But most of them just looked at Him as He was just another criminal crucified for His crime. Mankind did not understand what happened on Calvary that day.

The Bible says in Isaiah. 52, 14.
"As many were astonished at You - His appearance was so marred, beyond human semblance, and his form beyond that of the children of mankind."
It was not the human destruction and torture that made the Body of Jesus appear like it did there on the cross.
It was the battle that was going on in the spiritual world, which no human eye could see. Satan and the demons moved in on Jesus to conquer Him. Jesus let Himself voluntary be stricken by that which was rightfully intended for us.

The Bible says in Isaiah. 53, 5.
"Surely He has borne **our** griefs and carried **our** sorrows; yet we esteemed Him stricken, smitten by God, and afflicted. But He IS pierced for **our** transgressions; He was crushed for **our** iniquities; upon Him was the chastisement that brought US peace, and with His wounds **we** are healed."

Get "The stray dog" out -

The Bible says in Colossians. 2. 15.
"He disarmed the rulers and authorities and put them to open shame, by triumphing over them in Him."

This is Gods perfect victory, which has been given to you and me in His Son Jesus Christ.

Revelation. 1. 17-18.
Jesus says: "Fear not, I am the first and the last, and the living one. I died, and behold I am alive forevermore, and I have the keys of Death and Hades."

1. John. 3,8.
"The reason the Son of God appeared was to destroy the works of the devil."

And He did that 2000 years ago. This is mankind's only salvation. The Gospel of Jesus Christ, God Yahweh's living Son.

God's power to breakthrough.
If God's Word shall be living and powerful to change your circumstances – Then you have to believe that God's Word is alive in you!
You must have faith in what you do.

How will you get a faith like that?
If you are born again, you have it.

The Bible says in 1. John. 5, 4.
"For **everyone** who has been **born** of God
overcomes the world. And this is the victory
that has overcome the world—**our faith**."

**You don't feel it – you don't see it – but it
will work for you when you start using it.**

The bible says in Heb. 4, 2.
"For good news came to us just as to them,
but the message they heard did not benefit
them, because they were not united by faith
with those who listened."

You take God's Word, the Bible, and fill
yourself with it by reading it. You already
have the faith, as I already have mentioned.
It is born into you, in the new birth. But
either Gods Word or your faith will benefit
you if you don't act on it, use it.
The Word melts together with the faith in
your heart, with the faith in your spirit.
The word **faith** is verb, and all verbs are
describing an action taking place. For
example the verb *to walk*. It doesn't do you
any good standing in the street yelling: "I am

walking, I am walking", when you are not willing to move your legs and do what you say. Then your confession will have no meaning to you.

And with faith it is the same way. **Use your faith in God's Word by acting on it, do as God's Word says.**

Look at your circumstances as God sees them.

You might answer me and say: "Is it possible to see what God sees?" Yes it is possible for everyone.

Listen to what God's Word says in John. 1,1. "In the beginning was the Word, and the Word was with God, and the Word was God."

To see what God sees – is to see what Gods Word says.

The Bible says in 2. Corinthians. 3,18. "And we all, with unveiled face, beholding the glory of the Lord, are being transformed into the same image from one degree of glory to another. For this comes from the Lord who is the Spirit."

When we in honesty and sincerity fill
ourselves with the Word of God, and allow
the Word to work on us by obeying the
Word, we become changed to the same
picture that the Word gives.

**The change in the circumstances – will
always start with you.**

The Bible says in Matthew. 12,34
"Jesus said: For out of the abundance of the
heart, the spirit the mouth speaks."

**What do you talk about? What is your
spirit filled with?**

The Bible says in 1.Peter. 4, 11.
"Whoever speaks, as one who speaks oracles
of God."

The Bible says further in James. 3, 5.
"So also the tongue is a small member, yet it
boasts of great things.
How great a forest is set ablaze by such a
small fire!"
**If we fill ourselves with that which is
negative, then our speech will be negative**

Get "The stray dog" out -

**and create negativity. If we fill ourselves
with the Word of God, then we speak
Gods Word – and act on what we say, do
what the Word of God says. Then The
Holy Spirit creates what the Word is
saying. It gets created in our lives and
circumstances. Creating the positive.
Everything God creates, is positive.**

Here is an example on how the Word is
working. I was going to have a crusade in
Sudan and arrived in the country on the
appointed date. A native evangelist met up
with me at the airport. He told me that
nothing had been arranged. A civil war had
broken out in Sudan.
So, there I was – all the flights in and out of
Sudan got cancelled that same day.
The circumstances were screaming at me
through my senses windows: **This will not
work. You have lost, all hope is lost.** But I
stood up in the situation and said: **Stop in
the Name of Jesus!**

"He who is in me, is greater than he who is
in the world. We are of God, and have
victory over them (Satan and the demons)."
1. John. 4. 4.

It became an automatic reflex in my spirit
with God's victorious Holy Spirit in my
spirit, against the negative speech of the
circumstances which were being controlled
by Satan and the demons. I know that for a
steadfast Western man this sounds
unbelievable, but this is the reality either we
understand it or not.

**The negative got turned to positive in the
situation.**
How could this happen? It is because I was
filled by Gods Word, I had learned to obey
the Word. The victory was consciously taken
by me in Jesus Name in the Spirit. It resulted
in the changing of the physical
circumstances around me, after my
profession and action. Day number 2. and 3.
in Sudan, I preached in a Islamic culture
centre. And several hundred people gave
their lives to Jesus Christ, and many got
healed during these two meetings I had in the
middle of the civil war that had just started.
There were soldiers and gunfire everywhere.
On the 5th day in Sudan, an American pilot
had gotten permission to land with an
airplane delivering mail. He landed at the
airport which now was destroyed. I got in

Get "The stray dog" out -

contact with him, and he flew me from Sudan to Kenya, a flight lasting 4 hours.

There are so much more to tell about the trip to Sudan. It was full of experiences about victory over Satan's attacks in the world of the Spirit.

The meetings I held in the province capital Juba, Sudan, was the first ever. 30 years later some missionary friends of mine, that had a TV program about Sudan, told me that after those meetings the Gospel spread like a fire into all the nation. As a result of that, has 460 churches been planted in this Muslim nation, so far.

So you can see that when we FILL ourselves with the Word, and ACT on it – then we will after some time be rooted in it. Then acting out of God's Word will become more natural to us then to act out of our senses.

Everything impossible becomes to us a possibility.

The victory of Jesus Christ, was first and foremost a victory in the spirit world. It is the spirit world that is the primary world, so it is that world we got to relate to here in this secular world. People in the West have never understood this, but now is the time to make a change in the spirit and see the result in the physical world.

Chapter 23.

Throwing out demons.
The Lord has built up my life into a service
that works. There is nothing I have sought
after myself, my life has just little by little
become like this, starting in my youth. I
ended up as a preacher, yes, as an evangelist,
teacher, pastor and so on.
The things that have been natural to me all
these years are: Casting out demons, healing
the sick, people getting saved, proclaiming
the Gospel and teaching.
When the Lord leads you into service, then it
works, then you can manage all the tasks. It
is only in this way a service will come in to
function and work. When the origin is a
repented life totally given over to Jesus
Christ.

Got into this service without seeking it.
The service of setting people free from
demons, was something I just got into
without seeking it myself. I wanted to serve
Jesus with all my heart, and from that
attitude, tasks started to come my way. I took
hold of the challenges of the tasks, acted on
them according to the Bible, and gradually
got understanding and experience from this

kind of service. And from there it has been naturally to use this service all over the world.

Demons gets drawn towards The Holy Spirit.

In all the places I have preached the Gospel over the last 40 years, have those that were plagued with demons been like drawn to the meetings. This might sound contradictory, but those plagued by demons are like drawn to places were The Holy Spirit works.

I have received letters on the platform right before I were to preach, several times. They have been from witchdoctors who warns me and comes with threats. The hotels I have stayed at have gotten threats about attacks and arson. One of the times I also shared a hotel with a group of missionaries. They moved to another hotel when they got to hear about the threats.

Witchdoctors have been standing at some distance from the platform during the campaigns, and sent me threats through their agents. They have never liked meeting me face to face. Attacks with Molotov cocktails and stoning has also been done. These are some examples on how demons in humans react. This is a natural part of the offensive liberation service.

If the Demons reveal themselves to you, then you can throw them out.

Here is a very important point, many people want to "find, seek out" demons to throw them out of people. It doesn't work that way at all. I have been to meetings were I myself did not preach, but witnessed how persons have started some type of exorcism.

I have gone in and stopped séances. Outright abuse has been made against people, which have suffered psychological problems after such abuse. What has been done is actually punishable by law.

However, if you are in a setting were the demons reveals themselves to you, without you trying to "find" any, then you also have the authority to cast them out! They would not have revealed themselves to you, if you did not have had the authority.

When you have the authority in the situation, then you do like Jesus did. He cast out demons with one Word.

We command the demons to come out in Jesus Name! 1 time – Not 2 times.

If you do it twice then the second time is unbelief and doubt. Listen to what the Bible clearly says about those who doubt.

James. 1, 6-8:
But let him ask in faith, with no doubting, for the one who doubts is like a wave of the sea that is driven and tossed by the wind. For that person must not suppose that he will receive anything from the Lord; he is a double-minded man, unstable in all his ways.

A place in the Bible to mention, that takes on this exact thing is, when Jesus at one point came over to Greasiness and met 2 possessed men.

Matthew. 8, 29, 31, 32: "When Jesus came, the demons cried out, "What have you to do with us, O Son of God? Have you come here to torment us before the time?"

1. Here you can see that the demons revealed themselves to Jesus, He didn't have to look for them. We continue:

"And the demons begged him, saying, if you cast us out..."

Get "The stray dog" out -

2. Here we see that the demons knew they had to obey the authority. We read on: "And Jesus said to them, Go! So they came out."

3. Here we can see that Jesus gave a command with 1 word 1 TIME, and the demons went out. We see exactly what Jesus did and what was required. This is something Jesus did before the reconciliation, His death and victory at Calvary. His disciples did it also.

We live under the new covenant.
Now we are living under the new covenant, after Jesus reconciliation death and victory. The reality of this victory is given to the people which the Lord has given this mission. They have to repent and give their lives to the Lord and possibly be led into a service like this.
I mention repentance especially. If we that want to serve the Lord, and don't come to Him with a real and sincere repentance of our lives, we will not get born again. Even though many believe they do.
This is often the problem in "Christian congregations". They venture into spiritual realities, without repentance and without

being born again. What they then meet is just difficulties and no progress. Repentance to Jesus Christ out of a sincere and whole heart is absolutely necessary.

I have been teaching a lot at Bible schools through the years. The students have expected a lot of cheerful preaching and testimonies about miracles and deliverance. And that do I of course preach, but what I share the most is about a whole hearted repentance to Jesus Christ. I talk about the price we have to pay with our personal lives to possibly be led by God into a service like this.

The Lord leads you into a service, don't try it yourself.

In Philippians 3, 10 Paul says: "That I may **know Jesus Christ** and **the power of His resurrection**, and may **share His sufferings, becoming like Him in His death**,"

Here we see what is required to get into the position. **Revelation knowledge, yes, the relation** must come in place. Here Paul talks about your personal relationship, not what you have heard from everyone else, but **your** relation. You need relation to handle the task.

You will experience that **the power of His resurrection** comes parallel with you laying down your whole life to the Lord, and you experience to **share His sufferings**. You become more and more like Christ.
It is when Satan and the demons can see Christ in you that the magic starts.

One verse must in here – He was tested in everything like us, therefor He could be a better helper.

Listen further in James. 4, 7: "Submit yourselves therefore to God. Resist the devil, and he will flee from you."

Here you see clearly were your solid position must be – so you are able to do – Gods deeds.

"Religious Christians" can walk around in a "demon free world" with luck.
You can claim to be saved, born again, yes, a Christian. You can be completely sincere in your statements and in your wish to be born again. You attend Church every week, prayer

and worship. You can say: My whole life has been so "comfortable and blessed."

Are you born again?

But I have a question for you: Are you born again?

I believe we have to be willing to make a reflection on our lives, maybe after 10 to 40 years in a Christian fellowship, were things are "just old religious habits".

How is the spiritual life in you today? Have you ever been born again? Have you fallen out of the spiritual life in Christ?

Have you ever been baptized with The Holy Spirit, fire and power?

The baptism in The Holy Spirit is not speaking in tongues, but it is a baptism in The Holy Spirits fire and power. It is a Divine equipment to do God's deeds in the Name of Jesus, founded on the reconciliation work of Jesus Christ on Calvary.

Acts. 1, 8 Jesus told His disciples before He went back to His Father in heaven: "You will receive power when the Holy Spirit has come upon you, and you will be my witnesses." (Witness: Greek, martyr which means: One that puts down evidence to prove he is telling the truth).

1. Corinthians. 14, 4 and 14: "The one who speaks in a tongue builds up himself, but the one who prophesies builds up the church. For if I pray in a tongue, my spirit prays but my mind is unfruitful/without understanding."

Here we can clearly see what the baptism in The Holy Spirit is. It is baptism in the power of The Spirit for service. Speaking in tongues is for our own edifying, prophetic speech and The Holy Spirit interceding through our spirit.

Do you have The Holy Spirit's fire and power active in your life?
That is the big question.
The demons will never disturb you if you are "a Holy Spiritless, religious tongue speaking person". One that babbles some strange word with his tongue, which is not the same as baptism in The Holy Spirits fire and power. No demons will reveal themselves to you, nor are you in any position to throw any demon out.

However, if The Holy Spirit's fire and power are in your life, the demons will reveal themselves, because they feel threatened (which they are) when you come along. And you can throw them out. Even if demons reveals themselves to you, it doesn't necessarily mean you should throw them out, it all depends on the situation.

Are you not born again?

If you are not born again and starts "to mess" around with spiritual stuff, you can get grave problems bot psychological and physical. You open a door were you have no possibility to protect yourself. You are "lucky" if nothing bad has happened to you.

Get "The stray dog" out

Chapter 24.

Everyone that are saved can throw out demons.
This will work for you, not because you feel or understand it. The Lord wants you to know that this is for you.

We read in Mark 16, 17. Jesus revealed Himself for his scared disciples, who had gone into hiding after His resurrection. He first rebuked them for their unbelief and hard hearts. After that He gave them the great commission.
Further on He says in verse 17: "And these signs will accompany **those who believe**: in my name **they will cast out demons; they will speak in new tongues.**"

Now we're, you have received in faith, you have accepted and received, now you can use it in Jesus Name.

Who are the believers? 1 John. 5, 4 says: "For everyone who has been born of God overcomes the world. And this is the victory that has overcome the world—**our faith**."

The faith is yours in the new birth. When you have that, plus the baptism in The Holy Spirit's fire and power, you are ready for "victory battle" You will win every time. You can throw out demons every time they come your way. At this stage you have also got the wisdom to throw out, drive out, that which shall out.

How to throw out demons.
I remember a woman that was strongly bound in her personality by demons. This is many years ago, and I hadn't been Christian that long. She came to me for deliverance.

Yes
Before you are going to throw out demons, it is important to know if the person is willing to be saved, and that the person wants to be free from the demons. The person has to give his convincing "**yes**" to these 2 questions. If the person is not willing to give up his life to Jesus, then the demons will quickly return into this person, but this time 7 times stronger.

We read in Matthew. 12, 43-45: "When the unclean spirit has gone out of a person, it passes through waterless places seeking rest,

Get "The stray dog" out

but finds none. Then it says, 'I will return to my house from which I came.' And when it comes, it finds the house empty, swept, and put in order. Then it goes and brings with it seven other spirits more evil than itself, and they enter and dwell there, and the last state of that person is worse than the first."

We have to secure ourselves against Satan and the demons possibility to return.
I bind all the demons I meet today, in the Name of Jesus.
Before you get into the spiritual work with the person in question, you take a little "closet prayer". There you bind all the demons you will meet today in the name of Jesus Christ.
You declare that they are bound and tell them that they have to come out when you give the command. Then you worship the Lord loudly for the victory that has been prepared for us. This you do, and make sure that the demons can hear it, so that they understand that you KNOW that they have to flee.

You demon, you unclean spirit – Get out in the name of Jesus.

Now the demons might suddenly talk to you through the person in question, because they know the gravity now. Now they will try to manipulate and confuse you. They will have you to find out how many demons there are, and the names of them.

When you throw them out and you are bit insecure, then they just come right back. Then they start to say: "We are not coming out." They want to start a dialog on their premises. This is something you must never do! Never have a conversation with a demon!

You are the boss in Jesus Name, and they have to get OUT after one command. When you have given **one command**, then you have given one command, and they **have to obey**.

Whether you put your hand on the person or not, doesn't matter. Do what's best in the situation. This is the command that you give: "In the Name of Jesus Christ I command all you demons in this person to come out! Come out now in the name of Jesus! Amen." After some time with experience in this service, everything will go much smoother. The demons will not pop back in again, you will have control.

Resist Satan.
Before and during the prayer, the whole
woman was in an uproar because of the
demons.
After the prayer, I turned and went over to
another task about 5 meters away. I did not
wait to see the result, to me that would be
unbelief.
I had to let the demons understand that I
stood firm in what I was doing, by
commanding them out of the woman.

I was completely conscious about "having
the invisible in sight, and not the visible. For
the things that are seen are transient, but the
things that are unseen are eternal."
(2.Corinthians. 4, 18)

Of course I could have waited, but another
task was waiting a few meters away, and
because of that I might have been a little too
hasty. But it worked! While I were walking
over to the other task, the woman I had
prayed for walk the opposite way. Suddenly
I heard a loud scream! It was the demons
coming out of the woman, and she was free!
Here is the first secret I want to tell you:
When you have commanded the demons to
leave in the Name of Jesus, then you have

done it! If you are shaking in your pants and thinking that this might not work? But then, behave like the Word of God works through you! This you do consciously, with your willpower. Against all odds.

You see, Satan and the demons are watching how you are dealing with the situation. You must not let them see a shadow of a doubt in you, even if you are doubting on the inside. When they see you standing firm, they will leave! They might test your patience by delaying the departure.

Here comes another great promise into use. It is James 4, 7: "Submit yourselves therefore to God. Resist the devil, and he will flee from you."

It doesn't say how long we have to resist him, but we will resist him until he leaves. The promises are on our side, so hold on! When this have turned in to several positive experiences for you, then your faith in this task will grow and you will become determined and secure. It becomes easier for you after each time. Practice makes perfect. At the same time you get a stronger conviction of faith, (Heb. 11,1)

Get "The stray dog" out -

Satan and the demons becomes more and
more insecure about you. They start to fear
and respect Jesus Christ which is working
through you.
When I throw out demons from multiple
people simultaneously, it is in the exact same
way. They gather, or we have them gathered
at one place. When I come over to where
they are standing, the demons have already
started to come out.

Satan knows me.
I have done this so many times, and Satan
and the demons recognize me everywhere I
go. They know that they have no possibilities
to remain inside their victims. They know
that I KNOW that "Him who is in me is
greater than he who is in the world, Satan
and the demons."
When I come, it is not me they see, but they
see JESUS THE CHAMPION in me. This
right here is fantastic. This you can start
experiencing too. As I said: Practice makes
master, let Satan see The Master from
Calvary in you!

Get "The stray dog" out .

Chapter 25.

The inner backyard and the street outside – the spirit world inside you and around you.

In Oslo we lived in an apartment building, with backyards. We enjoyed ourselves in the backyards, but it was a regular battle against the enemies there. The enemies were the animals of the city. We thought all of them were fine animals, but they were enemies. And after throwing out the animals it didn't take long before they were back inside. One of the causes is of course all the ladies well-intentional feeding of "the poor animals".

As a grown saved man, I look at this as a picture of the battle in the spiritual world. If we look at the backyard as our soul, our personality, then every strange thing can sneak inside there. We did not have a gate into the backyard, so the animals just ran straight in, and inside they "got fed".

In our personality, our soul, we can be bound. If we don't have a closed gate into our soul. If we have a closed gate then nothing can enter. The same is with the backyards in the cities, if we would have had closed gates, then the "pestering" wouldn't get inside and make a havoc of everything.

When the gate was open and it also were being "served food to the poor animals" then the battle was lost that round. Here we got bound with ropes and chains, and the animals took charge in the backyard.

This is the exact same way as it is in the spiritual world. So fight, get "the stray dogs" out of your backyard's Oasis, together with all the other "snotty creatures". Then the backyard's oasis can flourish and the peace and harmony can settle in.

Let the creatures run on the cobblestone roads outside by the tram lines, until it all gets paved over, then they will go away from there also. Then Jesus has returned.

Get "the stray dog" out.

Get "The stray dog" out -

Chapter 26.

Reflection.
It has been exciting to write this book. I have put in something from my own childhood in the beginning of the book, and can clearly see that much of the spiritual activity in my life from early youth, took some great leaps forward, and increased in intensity in The Holy Spirit, from the time I got saved. It became a complete change in the spiritual life inside me and around me. It has been strange to see all that has happened in this period.

I have tried to bring up the most important things, but not the whole depth of the material. It would have been too much, and made it difficult to get a clear view and understanding, which I want you to have. One thing that you can clearly see now is this weaving of all the different religions, occultism, spiritism, New Age, Satan worship etc.

It is an endless conglomeration and everything is complicated.

The message of Jesus Christ from a to z, is easy to understand. Christianity is facing a lot of challenges in our time, and the Christians are "backing out". Christianity is losing terrain. The Bible clearly states that the victory is ours. And that is exactly what I want you to know through this book. No matter what Satan and the demons are bringing, what we have in Jesus Christ, is the eternal victory.

Soul-winning, liberation and healing ministry is a worldwide service. This is what I have put all my energy into since I was a young boy.

A local standpoint, with visions for the world. From where we are, we break all borders in in rhythm with the Bible, Gods Word!

Chapter 27.

20 – 20 vision.

Matthew 24, 14: Jesus said: And this gospel
of the kingdom, message of deliverance, will
be proclaimed throughout the whole world as
a testimony (word testimony is from the
Greek word martyr, which means to lay
down solid evidence to prove that one is
telling the truth) to all nations. You shall cast
out evil spirits, heal sick and proclaim the
year of the Lord's favour. This shall then be
preached, proclaimed, declared, announced
worldwide as a testimony, with evidence, as
a martyred, for all nations, and then the end
will come.(from Greek)

Acts. 20. 20: "how I did not shrink from
declaring to you anything that was
profitable, and teaching you in public and
from house to house."

Mass healing and mass deliverance.

As I have experienced in all the years of my
service for the Lord, namely: Are we in the
houses and heal and deliver among the few,
or are we on the town squares in big
meetings, there are a lot of healing and

deliverance. Then it is mass-healing and mass-deliverance.
It all "boils" down to the spreading of the Gospel's proclamation, so that Jesus can return.

Literature

A surch in secret India, Gsin & Borough press
Den kosmiske katedralen, Luther forlag
Der Gangesfloden flyter, Santalmisjonens forlag
Falne guder, Logos forlag, Kvinesdal
Guder og ledere i New age, Hermon forlag, Oslo
Hvorfor er jeg revolusjonær?, Richard Wurmbrand, Glendale, California 91209, U.S.A.
John of God, Cappelen Damm, Oslo
Kommunisme og religion i Sovjet Samveldet, Land og kirke forlag.
Kristus I vannmannens tegn, Credo forlag
Marx Satanist, Diane Books, U.S.A.
Mellom kors og halvmåne, Credo forlag, Oslo
Mennesket og mysteriet, Gyldendals - fakkelbøker, Oslo
Moderne trosretninger, Credo forlag, Oslo
Shan outreach centre, Oslo

Get "The stray dog" out

Sjelevandring, Lunde forlag, Oslo
Satan er løs, Logos forlag, Kvinesdal
Wikipedia, Internet

Books of Tom Arild Fjeld
Engelsks bøker
40 The mystery of the blood
41 Breakthrough in life
42 Pray through – prayer on the deep
43 He gave His life – no one could take it
44 Mystery
45 More than a conqueror
46 Get the stray dog out
47 The key to everything – faith
48 Victorious prayers of faith
49 Born again
50 Testimonies from around the world

Bøker til muslimer
51 Pilar of truth (to muslim)
55 Let god be God – to you (To hindu)

Tom Arild Fjeld has travelled the world around as a preacher of the gospel since his youth. The last years he has written many books, who is now coming out, the one after the other. They are actual books for the time we are living in. If you are follow social media, Christian tv stations and newspapers and see were he is preaching and teaching. Be a part of supporting his ministry regular financially, or be a part of the ministry. Follow the pages www.BrotherTom.org ,
Faith & Vision on Facebook and
www.twitter.com
Take contact on Facebook or on
www.tomarildfjeld@gmail.com
The account no. is: 0532.37.94229

Get "The stray dog" out -

Get "The stray dog" out -

www.ingramcontent.com/pod-product-compliance
Lightning Source LLC
LaVergne TN
LVHW051227080426
835513LV00016B/1456